THE
DIAMOND JUBILEE
BOOK OF SCOUTING

"FOUNDER AND SCOUT"

CONTENTS

[The Linking chapters were written by the Editor
The Scouting Proverbs by the Editor and Don Grisbrook]

OTHER DAYS

FOREWORD

by the Chief Scout of the Commonwealth
Sir Charles Maclean of Duart

WITH our Diamond Jubilee, Scouting is coming to the end of an epoch. This little book in a modest way celebrates the achievements of these sixty years during which Scouting has become established as a world wide Movement. In the next few years Scouting will see many changes because it must never lose its essential adventurous pioneering character. Its basic traditions will remain, but it must never be afraid to discard what no longer attracts contemporary boyhood.

It is not always realised how much thought and hard work goes into the production of a book like this; and I want to pay my tribute to its Editor, to the various contributors, especially that small representative band of distinguished old Scouts who have briefly remembered their Scouting on our behalf and by their remembering encouraged us all, to the photographers and the artists and indeed to everyone concerned with the book, not forgetting our own friends the publishers, who published *Scouting for Boys* all those years ago and have been associated with us ever since.

I hope that this book will be bought and read and cherished by old Scouts, by present Scouts and indeed, by future Scouts and I hope that many parents will buy a copy for their small sons as a souvenir of Scouting's first six splendid decades!

Charles Maclean

ACKNOWLEDGEMENTS

THE Editor wishes to express his deep gratitude to all who have helped in the making of this book; to the various distinguished writers, of course; to the cartoonists and artists, particularly Mr. Michael Jackson; to the photographers, especially Mr. Harvey Bennette for his frontispiece, to Mr. Neil Nimmo for his many contemporary photographs, specially taken, to Mr. David Cole, Mr. George Hoy and Mr. Peter Burton for their varied contributions; to all those at Scout Headquarters who so willingly assisted, especially to Mr. E. G. Wood and Mr. Jack Olden of the Publicity Department; to Mr. Jeffrey Irons who most kindly lent his splendid collection of County Badges for end-papers; to Mr. Len Rumble and Mr. Deryck Vesper who in conjunction with Mr. Neil Nimmo did the photographic lay-outs; and above all to Mr. Fred North, A.C.C. Hertfordshire, whose enthusiastic co-operation and generous assistance throughout has been invaluable.

PRELUDE

And what is sixty years when all is said,
That we should celebrate with conscious pride?—
Less than a life before its sands are sped,
Less than our dreams before their fire has died.

And yet for us this trifling span of years
Has meant hard striving and a ceaseless quest,
Doubt and frustration, triumph, failure, fears,
Great thought and care in seeking for the best.

And laughter, too, and fun and friendships made
Have lit the path, and precious cameos
Of golden days abide and never fade,
But leap and quicken as the firelight glows.

And boys we knew, now better men than we
Who led them, bear the burden of the day,
And lead in turn with splendid certainty
Their younger brothers on our chosen way.

For though the players fade regretfully,
The game goes on and on without an end,
Into the unknown mists of time to be,
While there are boys to serve who need a friend.

All that has gone before is just a chord,
The opening prelude to a mighty theme.
All the endeavour, all the work outpoured,
The mere unfolding of a future dream.

And others may, in greater times to be,
Look back at what we did, across the years,
And find we builded well and faithfully,
And say of us "These were the pioneers".

Hubert Blore

ACHIEVEMENT

"Not a patch on what it used to be"

WHAT IS SCOUTING?

I

"Six different things to six different people," said a wise colleague once.

"The aim of the Association," says Rule 1 soberly (in *Policy Organisation and Rules*), "is to develop good citizenship among boys by forming their character —training them in habits of observation, obedience and self-reliance—inculcating loyalty and thoughtfulness for others, teaching them services useful to the public and handicrafts useful to themselves—promoting their physical, mental and spiritual development." But gives no idea at all of the high spirits and high adventure, the fun and frolic, the colour of the spirit. For these—and for an answer to our question—we must go elsewhere:

Here perhaps from an artist friend of the writer's:—

"My first membership of a boy's organisation was the school Cadet Corps which I enjoyed well enough, but when a school friend encouraged me to join his Scout Troop I realised I had found what I was looking for: a society of boys that trained its members for the kind of adventures I had read about in books and had thought not within the reach of a timid, over supervised, suburban boy.

"To be trained to be self-reliant in the wilds, to be taught to see and understand all that went on there, to be able to put all one's needs in a rucsac and set off on the adventure trail: at that age I asked nothing more of life. I proudly wore the Scout uniform as the badge of an elite, but it was belonging that mattered, not the uniformity. My adventure book heroes had made their clothes from the skins of animals and so to be allowed to make my own woggle and my own knife sheath was a great delight.

"It was at a Scout camp that I saw my first sunrise, and it was like being at the beginning of creation. It occurs to me that many people must go through the whole of their lives without seeing a sunrise.

"Looking back at all my past companions, it is (as an only child) to the members of my Troop that I look back with the affection I imagine one has for one's brothers."

Or here from a Group magazine:

"We have just passed through the camping season and the boys have come home from week-end hikes and Summer Camp resplendent with badges; proud of their weariness and full of stories to make Mother gasp with horror and Father dream nostalgically of his own youth. They hiked alone, in pairs and in groups; slept out in home-made shelters of sticks and leaves; airily wrote off the hike tent as unnecessary weight; cooked fish on sticks over their camp fires; boiled custard in paper bags; collected their dessert from the berries in the hedgerows; crossed miles of country without touching a road, living as they never lived before. And the memories too, the things they will carry in their minds till they have children of their own to tell them to— sleeping under the stars on a Cotswold hillside with a clear spring bubbling nearby; striking camp by the light of a candle at 3 o'clock in the morning; tramping through a cold night under a brilliant sky."

Or here from another such:

"We congregated in the shade of the marquee for our Scouts' Own. The hymns were lustily sung, accompanied by R. on his squeeze-box and A. gave us a talk on facing failure which gave us all something to think about. Later, came the much-longed for night wide game, in which we had to creep silent and unrecognised past the cat-like eyes of Seniors and Scouters. We had a delightful Camp Fire next evening, and went to bed tired but happy, with the thoughts in our minds of this and other camps we had had, and of all those to come, where we can learn to live like brothers in our Great Scout Movement."

Here a boy writes in his log of an expedition:

"Most important of all it had been a time when the spirit of comradeship which there should be in every Scout Troop, was particularly prominent, and it is this spirit which makes or mars a trek, particularly when there are hard and difficult times to go through. . ."

II

Once it was an idea in the mind of a man of vision translated into an experimental camp on an island: Brownsea 1907!

One can sit on the quayside of pleasant Poole Harbour with the sun dancing on the moving water and stare at the Island—Branksea it was once called—dark and silent, and try to picture the scene with the men and boys—some no doubt phlegmatic, some excited—and to imagine the baggage and bustle of those summer days sixty years ago: and in one's mind's eye too one sees a slight, reddish, freckled, not very tall Edwardian gentleman, as lively as the sun on the water, the begetter of this quaint Edwardian adventure which was to reach out to touch millions of boys on the shoulder—Robert Stephenson Smythe Baden-Powell, welcoming with a smile the blithe, busy, slightly-bewildered boys as they landed.

There were, you will remember (including B.-P.'s nephew Donald) twenty-two of them: some public school sons of friends of B.-P., some local boys invited from the local Boys' Brigade companies: their parents had been reassured by the hero of Mafeking that "wholesome food, cooking, sanitation etc. will be carefully looked to" (and after the camp they were to receive a full report from him, too).

It is important to remember that these no doubt delightful guinea pigs were not Scouts—those still lay beyond the blue horizon. Still, during their ten-day camp they were Scouts in all but name, even though they didn't cater and cook for themselves, as Scouts would soon expect to do.

But they slept in tents, wore shoulder knots, yellow, red, blue, green—to show which Patrol (Curlew, Raven, Wolf or Bull) they belonged to, and a fleur-de-lis on their hats; they were taught the first elements of Scoutcraft—observation, stalking, first aid, firemanship and the like; they bivouacked at night, patrol by patrol; they sat round the camp fire as the flames leapt up and the stars came out and listened to tales spun by the great general, and sang songs he taught them. Once Scouting, one might say, was an island—and soon afterwards, it was a book.

III

Part 1 of *Scouting for Boys* appeared on the bookstalls on Wednesday January 15th, 1908: it cost fourpence. (That month a young man named Somers would be returning to New College and a Scots boy named Polson Corbett would be thinking of Eton.) The next five parts appeared on alternate Wednesdays during January, February and March; it appeared in book form in May 1908 at the price of a florin. Thousands of boys—unattached boys, boys that is who had for the most part not been attracted to cadets or youth clubs or the Boys' Brigade, were forming themselves into "Patrols", putting on unfamiliar "shorts", tying "scarves" round their necks, and with broomstick and haversack were doing their enthusiastic and excitable best to carry out the ideas of the magical book. A new sort of boy was about. In spite of the doubts of *The Spectator*, the boyish fancy *was* "captured by the precise mixture of seriousness and madness" which the book "prescribes as a working rule of life."

Scouting attracted the boys in the beginning because its ideas were novel: it offered the boys what no one else (and nothing else) offered them. They came to Scouting to get Scouting—and their minds hoped for the unusual, the adventurous, the romantic, the slightly crazy, the "legalised mischief", the wild woods and far hills of life.

Baden-Powell had taken the dreams of boyhood and changed them into realities.

The year went out in a great snowstorm, but a candle had been lit that no snowstorm could blow out, that the great hurricanes of two world wars could not extinguish. A candle had been lit which should light a million small camp fires in wood and meadow and by starlit streams, and around which joy and gaiety and friendship and brotherliness should flourish, and the boys of all free nations should smile at one another, and hold out their left hands.

IV

So it was an idea, an island, a book—a Movement (you can read its detailed history elsewhere in fuller pages than these: in B.-P.'s Scouts * and in Two Lives of a Hero *—both books which every Scouter alive should have on his shelves at whatever sacrifice and turn to again and again). And as a Movement it moved. The Sea Scouts came almost at once, and then the small brothers knocked imperiously at the Movement's doors and the Wolf Cubs leapt into being. Older Scouts stayed on to be known as Rover Scouts.

The Movement spread across the seas: already there were Scouts in Peru in 1910 (although no doubt they were English boys who happened to live there): and soon Scouts were sprouting everywhere.

"Why?" asked Mark Bonham Carter suddenly once, of the present writer "why was Scouting so successful? Why does it appeal to a boy in Pakistan equally with a boy in Peru? Why to the boy of this year as much as—or more than—the boy of 1908?" Or, as you might say "What is Scouting, that it so appeals to him?"

Well this is what it is . . .

It is a mixture of trying to live the good life (in some quarters a not very popular or admired quest today) and high spirited fun and friendship. It's a training in certain skills which help the Scout to help himself and others too in the emergencies that accompany life's common round. It's a growth in compassion for the less fortunate in mind or body or estate: any Scout Headquarters should be able to put across its entrance, the proud words "there are no strangers here". It's toleration: no one who has

* B.-P.'s Scouts (Collins 21/-); Two Lives of a Hero (Heinemann 63/-).

camped at a Jamboree and seen the thousands of Scouts of all colours and from many lands practising each undisturbed his own religion can doubt that. It's learning to read a map and tie a bowline and give the kiss of life; its playing a game called British Bulldog, and cooking a chicken on a spit, and building a bridge or a canoe and singing round a camp fire; it's gaining proficiency badges; it's a promise and a law. . . .

Sometimes, of course, it's not all this: its just a handful of dispirited kids held desperately together for all too brief a moment by what John Thurman has called "dedicated incompetence": but in a voluntary Movement which has overtones of brotherhood it is not easy to divest oneself of the weaker brethren. But at its best it is all that I have written above and much more. It is a game and it is very often a glory in the heart of a boy.

A mother wrote recently of her son: "I would like to say that although now only 14 years old, Scouting has played a major part in his life: he lives for Scouting"—as do thousands of boys the world over—but: what *is* Scouting?

It's a chosen way:

> "Now as I start upon my chosen way
> In all I do, my thoughts, my work, my play,
> Grant as I promise, courage new for me
> To be the best, the best that I can be".

MILESTONES IN
BRITISH SCOUTING—1

1907 July 29th to August 29th: *the Camp on Brownsea Island.*

1908 January 15th: *the first of the six fortnightly parts of* Scouting for Boys *published.*

April 18th: *The first issue of* The Scout *published.*

August 22nd to September 4th: *the camp at Humshaugh Camp: the first "national" Scout Camp.*

1909 May 3rd: *Scout Headquarters opened at 116, Victoria Street, S.W.1.*

July: *The first issue of The Headquarters Gazette (later in 1923 to be known as* The Scouter).

September 4th: *The Rally of 11,000 Scouts at the Crystal Palace.*

December 10th: *The Council and Executive Committee formed.*

1911 *The Sea Scouts came into existence.*

March 10th: *The first issue of Policy, Organisation and Rules approved.*

July 4th *The Windsor Rally of 26,000 Scouts reviewed by King George V.*

1912 *Royal Charter of incorporation granted by King George V.*

1916 *Wolf Cubs officially recognised.*

1917 *Scout Headquarters transferred to 25 Buckingham Palace Road, S.W.1, where for the moment it remains.*

1919 July 19th: *Gilwell Park opened.*

September: *1st Scout Wood Badge Training Course.*

1920 *First International Conference, London.*

August 6th: *B.-P. acclaimed Chief Scout of the World at the First World Jamboree held at Olympia, London.*

1922 June 14th: Rovering to Success *published.*

1925   December 5th: *First Scout Musical Festival held at Royal College of Music, London.*

April 3rd to 5th: *First National Rover Moot in London.*

1927   November 3rd: *The Chartered Associations (Boy Scout Association) Protection Order issued, giving legal protection to certain titles and badges.*

November 23rd: *Disabled Scouts branch officially recognised.*

1928   January 1st: *introduction of the Group system.*

1929   July 31st–August 1st: *3rd World (Coming of Age) Jamboree and Fifth International Conference in Arrowe Park, Birkenhead. Deep Sea Scouts scheme introduced.*

1932   October 31st–November 2nd: *First Gang Show held in the Scala Theatre, London.*

1934   April 22nd: *First National Scout Service at St. George's Chapel, Windsor.*

Gilwell Park presented to the Movement, 1919.

THE YEARS
HAVE GONE BY...

I

"If we all look back on the history of the past
We can tell just where we are"

as Sir Harry Lauder used to sing.

And where we are, just before our sixtieth birthday is with a vigorous and virile Youth Movement (more than half a million strong, of which over 232,000 are Wolf Cubs, 180,000 are Boy Scouts up to the age of fourteen and more than 62,000 are Senior or Rover Scouts in the fifteen to twenty-three age group: with over 63,000 Scouters and Commissioners) and which is notable for the way it has continually moved, as a Movement should, from the wintry mornings of 1908 till now. It may be added that there are more boys in Scouting today in the United Kingdom than in any other Youth organisation, more than in Youth Clubs and more than in all the other uniformed organisations put together. It may also be added that too many people think of Scouting as unchanged since it stepped ashore at Brownsea, or as something left over from Mafeking, with ideas and ideals hopelessly old fashioned: and they are wrong.

It is true that the Movement is old-fashioned to this extent: that it believes in self discipline and honour and loyalty and such

2   DJBS

unpopular virtues. It believes that a boy left to himself no more grows into a decent sensible adult than a plot of land left to itself grows into a garden. It believes that boys seek (and need) adventure and respond to a challenge. It believes that a love of the open air can enrich a boy's life; it believes that a boy who can look after himself wherever he happens to be is happier than one who can't. But as a Movement, it has always moved.

It is easy to think for example that the uniform is just the same but it isn't: one has only to look at the faded sepia snapshots of yesterday to see that. A Scout no longer feels undressed without a haversack over his shoulder and a staff in his hand. The original Scout hat, admirable for some occasions and unpractical for most, has been largely displaced by the beret which can be folded into a shoulder strap (it is interesting to recall that even on Brownsea Island B.-P. "was experimenting with a cloth hat that could be rolled up and stuck in the pocket"). Scoutmasters no longer wear breeches and Sam Brown belts! And other more striking changes have now been announced.

Once upon a time a Scout could gain a Silver Wolf on gaining twenty-four proficiency badges; now it is (and long since has been) the highest award for services to Scouting and is "the unrestricted gift of the Chief Scout".

In the early days every Troop had its trek cart and when Scouts went off to camp they loaded their kit bags and gear on to their carts and hauled away on the ropes:

"Over hill, over dale, as we hit the river trail
    and the trek cart goes rolling along.
    In and out, hear them shout, 'Gee I'm glad that
        I'm a Scout'—
    and the trek cart goes rolling along——"

Today few roads welcome a trek-cart and the danger outweighs the delight: coaches and cars and lorries and vans are available— and often Groups have their own.

There have always been developments in camping methods and Scouts have largely been responsible, led by Gilwell Park, the training centre given to the Movement by de Bois Maclaren after the First World War: someone once wrote that the Scouts invented good camping. Gilwell added a new dimension to Scouting: enthusiasts could become trained enthusiasts and

Gilwell brought to their notice wall tents instead of the old-fashioned and (for boys anyway) discredited bells; light weight hike tents; Swedish rucsacs ("Bergens") to own one of which became the passionate desire of every Scout and Scouter in the late twenties. And today Gilwell brings to the notice of Scouting new trends in tents, frame tents, mountaineering tents and indeed experiments constantly with the whole range of outdoor equipment. Gilwell opened windows and let in light everywhere.

A comparison of two camp programmes from 1911 and 1965 may be of interest. In the early year the daily routine was as follows:

6 a.m.	Reveille.
6.15.	Short drill by tent commandant for ten minutes or a double round the camp, halting at the flagstaff; prayers, saluting the colours, orders for the day.
6.45.	Tents cleared, ablutions, curtains brailed.
7.30.	Breakfast.
8.30.	Tent and kit inspection by officer of the day; fatigue parade for water, wood, kitchen, and clearing the ground.
10.0.	Scouting, drill, or classes of instruction.
12.30 p.m.	Dinner.
1.0.	Inspection of mess tins; boys free until 4.30.
5.0.	Tea.
6.0.	Inspection of mess tins.
6.30.	Camp games or night Scouting.
8.30.	Parade at flagstaff; prayers, salute, orders.
9.0.	Last post.
9.30.	Lights Out.
10.0.	Guard mounted, till 6 a.m.

And in camp earlier the same year:— "The time not taken up in cooking, washing up, and last, but not least, eating the aforesaid cooking, we spent in single-stick, boxing and quarterstaff bouts. These latter were great sport when using 8 ft. ash staves, gloves and helmets. We also had some ripping long-distance signalling from hill-top, the Morse flags (27 in. by 27 in.) looking more like 1 in. by 1 in. The Union Jack was hoisted and saluted each morning immediately after prayers, which were read at the beginning of the day's work."

They were (no doubt) golden days but they are gone. Turn to 1965. The 1st Aldborough Hatch which are a well-run but not exceptional church-sponsored Troop included in its camp programme:

"a cake and bread baking competition; athletic and swimming sports; a night incident; a fishing competition; pony trekking; Patrol pioneering (building an aerial run-way, a 26 ft. tower, a bridge and crane on a stream, rafts and a monkey bridge); a wide game; a commando course (rope bridge between trees, scrambling net, spar walk, rope ladder climb, log-carrying etc.); a moorland day hike for the younger boys, for the older boys a night obstacle journey; for the Patrols a competition which included baking, wood carving, backwoods cooking, painting with natural materials —and a pillow fight! One day the P.L.s were entirely in charge of the camp. One day there was a barbecue on the beach. One day the Patrols were sent out to find adventure. The whole camp was photographed and tape recorded and weather records were kept."

The only likeness between the divided years was that the boys were all Scouts and they loved outdoor activities.

It is the variety and imagination of the programme offered the Scouts that is impressive: and it is exactly this that has in the last decade or so made Scouting the modern Movement for boys that it is. Today opportunities for canoeing, rock-climbing, caving, mountain and moorland walking, and sailing and the like are everywhere. Many Troops construct their own canoes and since 1947 there has been an annual canoe cruise—on Wye, Severn, Avon, Thames, and Trent, every year but two. For years a winter expedition in Snowdonia has been organised to train Scouts in mountaineering and winter camping; the acquiring of Scout huts and hostels such as at Hag Dyke high on the Yorkshire moors or Hertfordshire's Scottish station at Lochearnhead has given the winter-wayfarers as well as summer adventurers bases from which to go forth exploring. The National Sea Scout Regatta allows the boys to show off their skill in swimming and boating. Caving has become so intriguing and appealing a challenge to so many Scouts that special training facilities (especially in Somerset) have been established to provide proper training and guidance. Endurance walkers have their annual Scout competitions in the Four Inns Walk, the Lyke Wake Walk, the Dalesman Hike and other such: these are most strenuous and nearly perilous expeditions which are not for the weaklings. For a long while British Scouts have supported the ski-ing courses centred on the International Scout Chalet at Kandersteg in Switzerland and now in their hundreds go to Scotland for the courses, Scout-run for Scout-skiers, there. For those Scouts who have a particular interest in cooking are held the National Cooking in Camp Competitions (in which they cook, to the amazement of the expert judges, such dishes as Escalope of veal Holstein, Beef Olives, Wiener Schnitzel, Filets of sole Duglère, Poulet à la grand-mère, to name a few). At Lasham Scouts own their own glider and gliding courses are oversubscribed. As a link with the past (and quite in tune with the modern vogue for smartness) an annual Scout Brass Band Contest was inaugurated in 1965. Camps with a purpose attract the older Scouts (to give but an example or two) to birdwatching in the Western Isles or to pony trekking in Norway or to cruising in our own inland waters or to orienteering (a combination of map reading, compass work and cross country running) on our wilder hills.

II

Every year nowadays between ten and twelve thousand Scouts camp, hike and visit abroad: no country of non-communist Europe is strange to them. Some Troops have gone beyond that—to the Atlas Mountains, to Nigeria, to Japan!—but these are exceptional. Many Troops are "linked" with Troops in the Benelux and Scandinavian countries or Switzerland or Germany.

Beyond this of course are visits to national camps by individual Scouts or Patrols—or of course the opportunities to represent Great Britain in the World Jamborees.

But more arresting, imaginative and challenging have been the national county or national projects abroad, of which the Essex, European and Explorer Belt expeditions can be taken as examples.

The Essex European Expedition, begun in 1950, has been held every third year, has provided adventure and experience in self reliance (and the chance to use their Scouting skills) for 1500 boys, who working from base camps they have established, hike in a strange country in groups of three, four or five boys for some eleven days, along a route they themselves have planned: during this time they are given special assignments designed to increase their knowledge of the country through which they are travelling.

Since 1958 the Explorer Expedition (belts are awarded only to those reaching the very highest standards of achievement: for the rest the journey alone must be their reward) based on the Essex prototype, has attracted hundreds of Senior and Rover Scouts. They have been held in Germany, Austria, Switzerland, and Sweden: they cover a wider extent of country; their requirements are more complex (each team of 2, 3, or 4 must specify and follow up a particular interest, e.g. forestry, architecture, heavy industry, education etc. as well as following a number of projects common to all).

But in our own islands Scouts have opportunuties for meeting Scouts from abroad in camps and by offering hospitality in their own homes. As long ago as 1946 the inspired vision of J. D. Stewart started Blair Atholl international camps, where Patrols from abroad camped and shared exploits with native boys: and variations of this have been held regularly since. The latest camp at Blair Atholl was attended by 100 Scottish P.L.s and a similar number of overseas P.L.s. It was a training camp for a week followed by a complete move to the Cairngorms for hiking before the boys returned to Blair Atholl and to enjoy hospitality in Scottish homes. Scouts from 36 countries have been at these camps over the years.

Counties such as Norfolk and Essex hold regular international camps which are enthusiastically attended. The latest of such camps as I write is Derbyshire's magnificently organised "Ramboree" of 1964 which was attended by 2,800 U.K., and 522 Scouts from Austria, Belgium, Canada, Denmark, France, Germany, Holland, Italy, Japan, Lebanon, Libya, Lithuania (exiles), Morocco, Nigeria, Norway, Sweden, Switzerland, Tunisia, U.S.A. Campers enjoyed archery, canoeing, adventure-hiking, rock-climbing, judo, horse-riding, sailing, gliding, parachute jumping from a tower, swimming, Morris dancing, swapped badges; held international tea parties, had Camp Fires where they taught one another national songs, dances and yells, constructed decorative gateways, compared camping and cooking methods.

During the second week overseas Scouts were guests in Derbyshire Scouts' homes.

It seems incredible that the general public in the light of all this tends still to think of Scouts as boys helping across the road an old lady who doen't want to go, or concerned with making fire by rubbing sticks together.

III

We record here our achievements: which does not mean that we are self-satisfied or uncritical or not conscious of problems unsolved. There have been missed opportunities: the inspired ideas of Voluntary Service Overseas and Community Service at home were the logical outcome of the Rover Scouts' motto of Service and although one is proud that a one-time Rover Scout Alec Dickson inspired both these great projects, that Scouting did not play a much more active and intense part in them is to be regretted.

In fact no satisfactory or enduring programme or plan for Rover Scouts has been devised, although several have been tried. Perhaps a Movement for boys and a Movement for young men are not happy yoked together. Undoubtedly Scouting has failed fully to live up to its noblest conceptions especially on service to the community although a service project was in 1964 added to the requirements of the Queen's Scout Badge. But much more is needed: helping elderly people, work with children in approved schools, the manning of road crossings, practising reafforestation, nature conservation, the learning of braille—all such should be considered part of Scouting's service if its training is not merely to increase the boy's capacity for self-dependence but to lead him to search for and undertake demanding service to others.

If Air Scouts had been inaugurated in 1928 (as B.-P. wished) Scouting might have attracted thousands of air-minded boys throughout the thirties.

As to our problems: in 1940 Lord Somers set up a "Post War Commission" to consider the development of Scouting and the achievements of the last quarter of a century are due in no small measure to his inspiration and the committee's wide-ranging thought, Now in the year of 1966 a similar commission of Scout younger statesmen known as "The Advance Party" appointed by another Chief Scout Sir Charles Maclean has reported and its ideas of how Scouting will be organised and how it will function are being vigorously discussed. Scouting has *never* stood still as the years have gone by.

MILESTONES IN
BRITISH SCOUTING—2

1938 The Boy Scout Fund launched at the Mansion House.

1941 January 8th: Death of B.-P.
January 29th: Lord Somers elected Chief Scout.
January 31st: Air Scout Branch formed.
April 16th: The Post War Commission set up by The Chief Scout to consider post war developments (Their report was published in The Scouter of July, 1942)

1944 July 14th: Death of Lord Somers.

1945 February 22nd: Lord Rowallan elected Chief Scout.
October 1st: Senior Scout section officially recognised.

1947 April 23rd: Memorial tablet to B.-P. unveiled in Westminster Abbey by H.R.H. The Duke of Gloucester.

1948 June 1st: B.-P. Guild of Old Scouts inaugurated at the Albert Hall.
October 1st–3rd: 1st National Representative Conference at Filey, Yorkshire.

1949 April 18th–23rd: First Bob-a-Job Week.

1957 Three commemorate stamps issued by H.M. Government to commemorate the 50th birthday of Scouting and the Centenary of B.-P. Ninth World Jamboree (combined with 3rd Indaba and World Moot) at Sutton Coldfield.
16th International Conference at Cambridge.

1958 August 1st: First British Explorer Belt Challenge, Germany.

1960 First National Cooking in Camp Competition.

1961 July: Opening by H.M. the Queen of Baden-Powell House, Queen's Gate, London, the memorial hostel to the Founder.

1964   *Setting up by the Chief Scout of an "Advance Party" to consider the future pattern, programmes and policy of British Scouting.*

1965   May 15th/16th: *1st National Father and Son Camp, Gilwell Park.*

      May 22nd: *1st National Scout Brass Band Championships, Coventry.*

1966   *Wolf Cubs celebrate their Golden Jubilee.*

1967   *The Boy Scouts Association celebrates its Diamond Jubilee.*

FOUR CHIEF SCOUTS
AND THEIR ACHIEVEMENTS

THE Scout Movement is peculiarly sensitive to leadership. Over the years it has been recognised that where there is success—where boys and young men, that is, have been helped significantly through Scouting to grow up with that combination of self-discipline and sense of social obligation we recognise as the Scout spirit, and which marks the mature citizen—the reason has been, not a particular badge test or type of uniform, not one programme of activities against another, not a big Troop as against a small one, but quite simply the quality of the man on the spot who lead the boys concerned. Where there has been a falling short, the deficiency lies not in the aims and methods of Scouting, which have stood the test of time, but in the character and vision of the Scout leader entrusted with the job of putting Scouting to work.

Right away let it be said, the type of leadership required is not authoritarian, or dictatorial; there is nothing relevant here of the officer–N.C.O.–other rank relationship; Scout leaders do not direct, or command. They have an infinitely more delicate and difficult assignment—to advise, to create opportunities, to encourage and help individual boys, to undertake the man-size job of training lying behind the boys' game, and above all by their lives and personal example to combine teaching with inspiration, to secure a unity of purpose in pursuit of Scouting's fundamentals while supporting every kind of diverse interest in every different sort of boy.

It is the great achievement of the four men who have accepted the role of Chief Scout that their personal qualities have measured up to these demands at the highest level in the nation, and that Scout leaders, and boys, have been proud to follow their distinguished lead.

LORD BADEN-POWELL OF GILWELL, O.M., 1857–1941
Chief Scout of the World 1920–1941

The Founder—and the only Chief Scout of the world, as the boys acclaimed him at the first jamboree, for that title died with him—was a man of astonishing vitality. His life has been vividly chronicled for us, first by E. E. Reynolds (*Baden-Powell*) and more recently by William Hillcourt with Lady B.-P. (†*Baden-Powell, the Two Lives of a Hero*). He was born on 22nd February, 1857 and so was fifty years old *before* his first experimental camp for boys to test out his ideas on Brownsea Island in the summer of 1907. His principal achievements begin then with two—first a full, adventurous and successful career as a soldier of the Queen, a Major-General at 43, and a national hero after the relief of Mafeking; and then, incredibly, the launching and leadership of what was to become the greatest of the youth Movements the world has seen, which he devised and guided from its unintentional beginnings in 1907–8 for over forty further years until his death in Kenya on 8th January, 1941 at the age of 83.

He lost his father at the age of 3, but his upbringing with his family, and his schooling at Charterhouse were both fortunate. The great age of Victoria was the setting for a family who sought to serve God and country, and his mother taught him a sense of purpose and gave him great strength of character. Through his activities with his brothers, he looked wide on a world which was to become very wide for him indeed. His wise headmaster "allowed both boys and masters the largest measure of independence". Here were the seeds of Scouting. His career in the

* Oxford 1942;   † Heinemann 1965

army began in India where, both then and again 20 years or so later, he introduced an unorthodox training for young soldiers in reconnaissance, or scouting, involving in particular the trusting of young leaders by the method of "brief and then delegate", and inculcation of the basic skills of living in wild country—personal hygiene and first aid, route-finding by day and night, observation, nature lore, camp-craft and pioneering—and devised a badge consisting of the north-seeking point of the compass as the mark of those proficient in showing the way. Here was the recipe which later provided the basic programme of a great game for boys.

His personal success was spectacular. He hated hidebound rules and unintelligent drill; he exulted in unusual tactics and techniques, in adapting himself to new localities and new colleagues; he was a master of improvisation, and his organisation and leadership at Mafeking was a classic demonstration. Here were the imagination, the breadth of vision, the personal fearlessness (of authority and the enemy alike!) and the sense of fun which made his leadership irresistible, and here were the qualities which endeared him to youth leaders and young people for a generation.

Now came the next achievement—the flexibility of mind to effect an easy and logical transition from the arts of war, first to the peaceful and highly effective organisation of the South African Constabulary, and then to the founding of Scouting for Boys, by recognising—as so many critics of the early days of the empire and of B.-P. failed to see—that there are qualities which are timeless in men and appropriate to changing circumstances. He himself regarded his work in the Constabulary as his best. But what imagination was his when he drew on his exciting and full life to write a few magazine parts, to give the youth organizations of his day a more attractive programme and so unintentionally started Boy Scouting and World Scouting.

What followed was so astonishing that to single out facets of his career as individual achievements would be to ignore the immense total result. A social anthropologist who has studied the influences which separate men—language, colour, creed—and those which tend to unite them—medicine, music and the rest—put the Scout Movement high up on the second list. It was genius to devise the basic principles of Scouting so simply and timelessly that they have found acceptance in every continent and among all the peoples of the earth. The formula of characteristic adventurous activities in the open air, training in small units under trusted boy leaders, and the underlying moral code of the Scout promise and the law, have stood the test of time and distance, and have proved capable of infinite variation and modernisation without losing its core. This was achievement indeed.

His personal contribution to the spread of Scouting throughout the world was incalculable. He remained active throughout his life in producing new ideas and suggestions. He was tireless in travelling and speaking, in writing in *The Scouter*, and particularly in the boys' magazine *The Scout*, and he was spared for so long that the foundations of the Movement were well and truly laid. He was a master of delegation of responsibility, and of the art of making people want to work for him. He was personally responsible for the inspiration which created one of the greatest demonstrations of voluntary service the world has seen. Having written the basic handbooks, he established his leader training system—again on unique and highly effective lines, the Wood Badge course—so that his volunteer leaders, first of his own country and thereafter of all countries, might see and take part in a live demonstration of Scouting's activities, method and spirit. He travelled overseas to the dominions and colonies and abroad to foreign lands. His utter sincerity and personal integrity made him a national and international figure. He was awarded the rare and distinguished Order of Merit in 1937 and no less than 20 foreign orders. His memorial stone is in Westminster Abbey, mark of his numbering among those who have made this nation great, but to quote a reference to an earlier celebrity "Si monumentum requiris, circumspice"—if you seek his memorial, look around you; World Scouting—with ten million members in more than eighty separate countries.

It was once said that the history of our land is full of the stories of great men, most of whom alas were dull; then there are the engaging characters who appear, but unfortunately most of these are irresponsible. Once in a while, however, there comes on the scene a great character, and such are the salt of the earth. Lord Baden-Powell of Gilwell, O.M., was one of the world's great characters. He achieved true happiness through giving it to others, and his work goes on in the hands of a creative minority, to put it no higher,—those Scouts past and present and the many millions still to come whose combined goodwill may well speed the day when nation shall speak peace unto nation.

Lord Somers, 1887–1944
Chief Scout, 1941–1944

The death of the old Chief in Kenya in the darkest days of the war imposed serious problems; his successor had no opportunity except in a holding operation. No one knew what the effect of the war might be in this country or across the seas. No one knew whether the Founder's death would result in disintegration of the Movement or the loss of the binding qualities of Scouting's fundamentals. Superposed on these uncertainties was the acute personal problem of succeeding B.-P.

Fortunately, the Founder in 1936 picked a deputy in whom he had trust—whose personal attitude to life, to self-discipline and to service, and whose ability to inspire others, were attuned to his own beliefs and talents. He too had been to school at Charterhouse, and had a distinguished record in the services, in the less glamorous but more devastating conflict of 1914–1919 where he was awarded the D.S.O. the M.C. and the Légion d'Honneur. He too had travelled in the commonwealth countries. Lord Somers rose to be Governor of Victoria in Australia in 1926–31 during which time he was a very active State Chief Scout. He went on to act as Governor General for two years. He was devoted to cricket and as President of the M.C.C. he toured with the test team in 1936–37.

But it was in the London of the blitz and the Britain of the build-up for the invasion of Europe that Lord Somers was faced with his difficult task. As the emergency grew, he had given clear direction that the Movement's duty lay under two heads—to continue with training Scouts, and to give practical help in every possible way. He gave consistent leadership and guidance during the period when Scouts assisted in civil defence and in countless other ways. Later, under his guidance and with great foresight, the courageous step was taken of setting up the Post War Commission, composed of experienced Scout leaders from all parts of the country, who produced a report and recommendations designed to help Scouting to take its place in the post-war world. This proved to be an indispensable part of the Movement's story. He also launched the Memorial Fund for B.-P. which in good time gave us the splendid Baden-Powell Memorial House, the International Scout Hostel in London.

Meantime, the new Chief travelled so far as conditions would allow, meeting leaders and boys. Everywhere he inspired deep affection, particularly at headquarters in London where his personal influence on the staff was quite outstanding.

He never had the reward of the days of peace and expansion. He suffered an increasingly painful cancer which affected his speech and eventually caused his death. His devotion to his duty and his constant triumph over pain and anxiety were the abiding memory of those whose fortune it was to meet with him and work with him. His great potential achievements were denied him, but his success was in holding the Movement together after the Founder's death and turning its eyes from looking backwards to the more challenging and demanding days ahead which he was never to see.

Lord Rowallan, b. 1895
Chief Scout, 1945–1959

Strangely, the writer's first contact with both Lord Somers and the next Chief Scout was at the Third World Rover Moot in Scotland (at Monzie—the 'z' is silent!) in 1939 where Lord Somers spoke most movingly at the Camp Fire and again at the International Conference dinner in Edinburgh which followed. At the Moot's beginning, the then President of the Scottish Council and County Commissioner for Ayrshire, Lord Rowallan, read the French translations at the torch-passing opening ceremony. His unusual Cameron kilt, his commanding figure, and his powerful and musical voice made him a prominent figure in fact, if not yet in national and international reputation at that time.

When the Great War broke out in 1914 he was 18, and went straight from Eton to the army—Gallipoli, Egypt, Palestine. There was an M.C. for personal gallantry and a serious leg wound. Then came years building up his family estate in Ayrshire, specialising in pedigree dairy cattle, chairman of a major commercial company, governor of a bank—and service to the community in farming and other fields. He was a T.A. officer too, and raised and trained a new battalion in his county with whom he went to France in 1940, narrowly escaping capture in the fall of France. He had met B.-P. as a wee boy, and had read *The Scout* from the beginning. He became a D.C. and C.C. and then President for Scotland.

Now came a fusion of his Scout and services experiences—strangely reflecting B.-P.—when he used Scout methods in a special Young Soldiers' Battalion for boys who had been in trouble, with remarkable character training results, and later at an army school in the highlands he again achieved impressive results with potential officers requiring further training. And so it was that the third Chief was a kilted Scottish laird, business man, ex-infantry officer, and Scout Commissioner, who had already given exceptional service in all these capacities when he was asked to succeed Lord Somers.

From then on, there was little time to spare at home to indulge his love of pictures, music, reading, shooting, or his hobby of cinematography at which he was expert. He travelled the equivalent of eight times round the world, visiting all the great dominions and nearly all the colonies and dependencies and mandated territories, and he visited Scouting in Europe and the United States. He attended the World Jamborees in France in 1947, Austria in 1951 and Canada in 1955, in England in 1957, and the Philippines in 1959 to lead the Commonwealth Scouts. As a world figure he received—most appropriately—the K.B.E. in 1951.

Apart from the major tours and events, he travelled up and down the land giving direct leadership and encouragement, ranging from his presence on the Committee of the Council to shaking the left hand of countless Wolf Cubs at rallies. And he served on the International Committee, the executive body of World Scouting.

Magill University in Canada and Birmingham and Glasgow in this country made him LL.D., in acknowledgement of his outstanding contribution to citizenship. In 1957, Scouting's great celebration of the Founder's centenary and the jubilee of the Movement, he became a freeman of Edinburgh, and his personal distinction, devoted leadership and example which had contributed so much to the Scout Movement's redevelopment after the war years, was recognised by the Queen, who appointed him to be a Knight of the Most Ancient and Most Noble Order of the

Thistle, Scotland's highest Order of Chivalry, again a most appropriate decoration for one who lead a Movement which the Founder had always visualised as an order of chivalry for boys in modern times.

M.C.—a gallant officer; LL.D.—a distinguished citizen and servant of the community; K.B.E.—an outstanding leader in the commonwealth and empire; K.T.—a Scotsman of the first rank.

A press profile said of him "as a speaker he is a spellbinder—perhaps his greatest gift" (when Scouting took a stand about admitting as a leader of boys a member of a political party dedicated to the destruction of voluntary youth Movements and of personal freedom in religion, he delivered a speech in the House of Lords about which it was said "in fifty years, I have never heard a case so torn to shreds and tatters that it ceased to exist"), "a man with the highest sense of duty to God and his neighbours, a real love of boys, with high standards of efficiency in everything he puts his hand to, and above all a good companion. He is a much loved man, happy in the knowledge that in an age of doubt his life's work is gaining momentum".

His achievement then—to be the sort of Chief Scout we needed in the post-war world, who saw the great period of anxious experiment and re-establishment through to the peak of the jubilee year which found Scouting in good heart and in high regard abroad. On 6th September of that year, he handed over to his successor—the first Chief Scout to be able to do so—and went on to become Governor of Tasmania for a spell before coming home to continue his active interest in Scouting.

Sir Charles Maclean, b. 1916
Chief Scout, 1959

Inevitably, as the first fifty years ended and the glamour and excitement of the jubilee year's events faded, there was a sense of anti-climax. But there was more than that; the public interest in the Youth Service resulted in searching enquiry into the needs and aspirations of young people. In an age of penetrating analysis and criticism Scouting came under acute review—not only in the United Kingdom—and its fundamental principles came under question in many quarters. These conditions called for a leader of quite exceptional calibre. He had to be a leading citizen, or Scouting's place in the community might be imperilled. He had to have faith in Scouting's principles, but a youthful and sensitive mind to admit and welcome change in details. He had to be acceptable to the traditionalist and yet to inspire and encourage young leaders and boys in a period of unprecedented change and progress. He had to be acceptable to the leaders of a rapidly evolving and expanding commonwealth of Scout-recognised separate countries. He had to be a boy's man and a leader of men. These contrasting requirements, needing determination and tolerance, enthusiasm coupled with patience, seemed to specify the impossible. But he was found, and Sir Charles Maclean, Bt. became twice a Chief, for he was 27th hereditary Chief of the 40,000-strong Clan Maclean.

He lives in Duart Castle on the tip of Mull off the west coast of Scotland—an historic keep built in 1365. He is the Lord Lieutenant of Argyll and so it was he who greeted Her Majesty the Queen when she came ashore at Iona from the royal yacht on the post-coronation cruise in the Western Isles.

During the war he was commissioned in the Scots Guards and in the invasion of Europe saw service in France (landing on the Normandy beaches) Belgium, Holland and Germany.

He was County Commissioner of Argyll and Chief Commissioner for Scotland, and gave notable service to Scottish Scouting; it was to their mixed regret and delight that this much loved man, farmer and cattle breeder, lover of music, interested in ski-ing, royal tennis, hiking, shooting and squash—and in travelling which was just as well!—gallant officer and outstanding Scout leader, became Chief Scout of the United Kingdom and overseas branches, and later, at a conference in New Delhi of delegates from the independent countries, Chief Scout of the Commonwealth.

He came to his high responsibility, then, with very similar attributes of standing in the community, of service to his country, and of experience in the affairs of town and country, as his predecessors, but above all he came with a sincere and personal faith, and a belief in the value of Scouting which he communicates to all with whom he makes contact. His willingness to identify himself with the Movement's work at this time showed perhaps more moral courage than was demanded of those he succeeded.

His first great achievement has been to win respect, affection, and devoted loyalty at a most difficult time. He has a quite exceptional gift in dealing with people; he will walk with royalty on some great occasion or on a personal visit to his home, and chat to the delight of both with a young Cub on one of his countless tours and visits. He will inspire a national conference from the platform, and a few minutes later will disappear, to be discovered in an obscure corner, arguing out some point with a group of young leaders as though he had known them for years. He has wisely listened before speaking, wisely kept out of the hurly-burly of debate about the Movement's organisation and programme, but firmly maintained its eternal truths.

He has undertaken an extensive and comprehensive series of commonwealth tours covering all the great dominions, the new nations in Africa and the Far East, the islands of the Carribean the Mediterranean and the Pacific. It is not possible to calculate the measure of goodwill created by this unassuming but compelling man, winning respect for Scouting's principles and setting the seal of personal integrity on the work of the Movement he so magnificently presents to the community in this country and abroad.

Keenly sensitive to trends of public opinion and to the risk of Scouting as a uniformed and authoritarian youth Movement losing contact with today's young people, Sir Charles set up a commission, significantly of young leaders exclusively, with an unlimited brief to investigate with all means at their command the fundamentals and details of the moral code, programme of activities and training method of Scouting, a committee appropriately called "The Advance Party" whose brief was to report to him personally without fear on their recommendations for changes and developments desirable to equip the Scout Movement to serve the 1970s and the years ahead. At the time of writing this, the work of The Advance Party is about to emerge in the form of a report to the Chief Scout, which he will personally present to the Committee of the Council, and it will be a matter of the greatest interest both in this country and in all the Scouting countries overseas to discover what must be changed and what must be retained if Scouting is to continue to serve the boys of all countries. One thing is certain; the principal achievement of the present Chief Scout has still to come when these promises come to be implemented and when, as always in Scouting, the drive and the example and the faith must come from the leader.

The Founder, then, gave a priceless gift to the world through his creation of Scouting for Boys. The outstanding achievement of Lord Somers was his reminder that the essence of Scouting lies in the spirit of those who serve and those who are inspired by that service. Lord Rowallan rose magnificently to the need for strong leadership and guidance in the post-war period of redevelopment and experiment. Now Sir Charles, with a magical combination of modesty and firmness, taking his task seriously but always enjoying—and transmitting,—the fun in the game of Scouting, has established his position like an orchestral conductor who knows that there is a powerful and impressive climax in the score of his symphony and so keeps something in hand in his team of players, so that the impact of all the work of rehearsal and preparation will not be spoiled when the great moment comes.

How wonderfully these four men matched the call of Scouting to the needs of the time in which their service came. How wonderfully all four have grown in stature in the job they did and do. The Scout Movement is profoundly grateful for their separate and total achievement.

THE COMING OF
THE CUBS

The Wolf Cubs were recognised as existing officially in 1916. As early as 1913 a programme had been outlined for "Junior Scouts" although B.-P. said that name would never do: he had in mind something like Colts or Beavers or—Wolf Cubs. In The Headquarters Gazette *(later* The Scouter) *in January 1914 a scheme was outlined for "Wolf Cubs or Young Scouts". But the scheme was only watered down Scouting and B.-P. was not satisfied. At this time B.-P. went to live at "Ewhurst Place", Bodian, East Sussex; Rudyard Kipling was living at "Bateman's", Burwash quite nearby, and they were in constant touch by letter and visit. It is therefore quite natural that the idea came of using the great Jungle Books as a background for the new venture and equally natural that Rudyard Kipling was delighted to give his consent. The first Cub Conference took place at Headquarters on Saturday 24th June, 1916 when B.-P. outlined the new scheme.* The Wolf Cub's Handbook *was published on December 2nd, and the first Wolf Cub display ever took place in the Council Chamber of Caxton Hall, Westminster, on Saturday December 16th. The Wolf Cubs had arrived! And their numbers grew rapidly.*

They had two "great days" in 1922 and 1924. On Saturday October 7th, 1922 they played their part in The Posse of Welcome *arranged to welcome H.R.H. The Prince of Wales (later the Duke of Windsor) on his return from an Empire tour: of them B.-P. wrote "Those hordes of imps of enthusiasm, the Wolf Cubs (19,000 instead of the 10,000 we had expected) with their throat-gripping Howl and spontaneous cheering was perhaps as moving a feature as any in the day." Mr. Kipling was there.*

In 1924, on Wednesday August 6th, Wolf Cubs had their own day at the Imperial Jamboree at Wembley when the Duke of York (Later King George VI) was present: since then the Cubs of the host country have normally had their special day at World Jamborees. I remember writing about this in 1947: "Monday was the day of the Louveteaux in their dark blue shorts and crossed braces and sky-blue shirts and dark berets. It will be difficult to forget a vast circle of 1200 of them all turning head over heels at once."

Cubs are Cubs, the world over.

In 1966 they celebrated in our own country their 50th birthday and in no uncertain fashion. They crammed into a special Jubilee performance of Mr. Mills' circus; they made scrap books on their Cub life for Cub Packs overseas and sent them birthday cards; they undertook a vast national good turn collecting silver paper for Guide Dogs for the Blind as well as local good turns at Eastertide; they had a special Pack Meeting on Saturday June 4th and their own musical pageant play with 800 Wolf Cubs taking part in the Albert Hall, London on June 25th.

" Hello, Brother Scout."

THE YOUNGEST MEMBERS

THE noisy ones, the unpredictable ones, overflowing with energy and enthusiasm, liable to spoil everything and guaranteed to catch the public eye: those Cubs.

Most people know the story of the "boys who were too young", the boys who, in the early days of Scouting, bombarded the nucleus of Troops like neutrons, many of them breaking through the barriers and upsetting the balance of the Patrols with 10-year-olds for whom Scouting was not intended and was not suitable.

Jungle Wisdom by Vera Barclay, tells how the Founder met this challenge, not by embargoes or by formulating a "holding brigade", as many people believe, but by a new set of ideas and ideals, to which he gave his whole attention and his inimitable flair for meeting demand with exactly the right supply. For "he was convinced"—and I quote from *Jungle Wisdom*—"that a boy can't start his Scout life too early".

He also knew that "a full programme is the secret of success", and for this purpose he wisely consulted, at a Conference in June 1916, those Troop Scouters who were already suffering from the effects of the Scouts who were too young. From these he selected Vera Barclay as the one to formulate experimental tests and to work out an appropriate scheme of training, planned especially to keep the 8-11 age-group busy and therefore happy; to segregate them from Scouting but, all the time, to prepare them for the Troop, so that they might be ripe and ready when the time came.

But the inspiration of the Jungle background, the adaptation of it to our needs, and with it the wording of the Cub Law, the action, noise and symbolism of the Grand Howl, was all his own, and shows his extraordinary understanding of small boys as well as bigger ones. These basic principles and methods are now accepted and wholeheartedly approved by the child psychologist of today, who acknowledges B.-P. as a genius fifty years ahead of his time.

It is the Jungle which is most often the target for criticism, but nobody has thought of another background which would combine such colour and atmosphere with so many underlying examples of loyalty, team spirit and obedience to an acceptable law. These the Cubs absorb into their systems along with the fun and excitement. The most ardent critic, too, would not like to sacrifice the title "Akela", which symbolises the very special relationship between Scouter and Cub.

As a background, once established, properly used and kept in proportion, the Jungle is, in my opinion, irreplaceable and leaves room in the foreground for any amount of variety and up-to-the-moment activity.

On this foundation Cubbing has grown, both in size and scope, and still, as from the beginning, the Scouters who are working with Cubs have their say and express their opinions, which have effected many minor changes over the years. Headquarters, with its manifold departments and complications, has had to grow as the Movement grew, but all those concerned with Policy and Administration are themselves Scouters, experienced in their particular field but with the well-being of the Movement as a whole as their first concern.

With a quarter of a million Cubs in the British Isles alone, there are of course considerable variations, both in demand and in application. What suits Packs in the Isle of Skye may not suit those in the Isle of Wight. It is for Headquarters to achieve a fair and reasonably elastic balance to suit them both, and all their brothers in between from Donegal to Skegness—particularly Skegness, perhaps, where their voices are most vociferous. And now that Cubbing has spread to so many other shores, the variations and a certain amount of healthy competition have increased.

We can all learn from each other: from the Cub Scouts of America, maybe, the importance of including the family; from Canada perhaps the value of a set of projects, particularly out-door ones; from the Welpen of the Netherlands something of the practical out-door fun of the Jungle; from Malaya the adventurous nature of their programme. This is a random selection and not intended to be invidious, for one only has to meet Cub Scouters from the five continents to realise the adaptations that are necessary and the common purpose that unites us. This perhaps is crystallised in the Founder's own country, where we may show the world a loyalty to those basic ideas and ideals which have stood the test of time, combined with a width of vision in keeping Cubbing up to date and, all the time, in line with the developments of Scouting.

It is evident that we must move with the times and step up Cubbing to match the Cub-aged boy of today, who is, in some respects, so much older than his Dad and his Grand-dad were. But only in some respects.

At the Open Cub Day at Gillwell one gets an idea not only of the size of the mass but also of the individual. With every wonderful device laid on for their entertainment, one may see small parties defending a ditch for a happy hour, with sticks and loud war-cries; while hundreds of others besiege the 'I Spy' bookstall thirsting for information on an incredible variety of subjects from Aircraft and Antique Furniture to Zoology, and thousands are queueing for the Aerial Railway and Scout-like adventure. But there are many who claim that the best part of a wonderful day is sitting round a camp-fire after a swim and devouring enormous slabs of bread and jam. It is usually, in my opinion, these simple things which delight them most, and would equally have delighted my Cubs of fifty years ago.

One may assume, then, that the Cub of '66 is more of a mixed-up kid than the Cub of '16. Certainly his mind is more elastic than it used to be: there are many more stretching agencies and, perhaps, many more stresses and strains under which elastic may snap unless it is reinforced with stronger material. The boy's opportunities, experience and general knowledge are much greater than they were, but fundamentally he is Boy, just as performing animals in a circus are fundamentally Bear and Elephant and cannot ever be anything else. And thank God for it, because basic Boy, before the mixing-up effect of puberty, is essentially a thing of sound and simple delight, of straight dealing and ready response to any lead.

The secret of the success of Cubbing is that it caters for the natural instincts of Boy, giving him what he needs and what he wants, which in other fields of education often seem to be diametrically opposite, and for which only a genius like B.-P. could find the formula. That must continue to be the key to Cubbing in the future: it must go the way the boy is growing, adding to his natural fun, bringing out the best that is in him and helping him to make the most of his opportunities and his gifts.

We must go with the current of contemporary development, using it for our own good purposes rather than pulling against the stream. But with the same sure foundation of the Law and Promise with its habit-forming steadfastness which is more important than ever. The "full programme" must be active, exciting and challenging to both mind and body, but all the time streamlined with Scouting, so that when the boy goes up he may continue with the same forward impetus.

Nowadays there are fresh problems to complicate the programme planning. It must cater for the two extremes: the boys who are not wanted at home by parents who are too much preoccupied with their own work or amusements or troubles; and the boys who are given everything they could desire, on a dangerous tide of prosperity. These, and all the individuals in between, must be made to feel that they are wanted, that they are committed to a family way of life with a job to do, a sense of purpose and a tremendous enjoyment of those early, glorious years.

The problem of catering for the older Cub is also more pressing than it used to be, since statistics have shown that more boys leave the Pack, and therefore the Movement, after ten years old than at any other time. At this age they need more attention, more of a progressive, challenging programme than the younger boys, who are carried along on a wave of indiscriminate enthusiasm. The enormous in-take of eight-year-olds is no credit to Cubbing, since they would just as gladly join a troupe of performing sea-lions. But they wouldn't stay with them long once they had plumbed the limitations of the pool and tired of a fish diet. They need to explore wider fields and a variety of expanding interests. It is this holding power which is the test of Cubbing. Cyril

Fletcher summed it up for us, apropos something quite different, when he said: "It is a pity to curdle the cream in an effort to coddle the clot."

The material is as magnificent as ever it was, and Cubbing has been tested and proved to be the right tool, if it is properly handled, tempered with imagination, ground with sharp vision. And the greatest of these, perhaps, is imagination, without which one cannot capture or hold the elusive boy.

But imagination doesn't necessarily mean wild flights of fancy and crawling about on the floor. It is often the gilding on the pill, or the magic that transforms penny-plain into tuppence-coloured. Nor is it entirely the preserve of the Cub Section. Cubs need realism just as much as Scouts do, and all Scouters need imagination in presenting their realistic projects, and plenty of realism to make the best of the imaginative activities.

One can learn a tremendous lot from the boy himself. When he was Chief Scout, Lord Rowallan told a story about a large gathering of Cubs to whom he was to speak. It took a little time to get them all sitting quietly, but still he paused a moment before saying "I'm just waiting till the two boys at the back have finished fighting". He had not realised, he said, that every Cub in the place would promptly surge to his feet and crane his neck to watch the fight.

The taste and capabilities of the adult vary much more than those of the individual Cub. When an Akela states, for instance, that his or her boys don't like yarns, it is reasonable to assume that that Scouter is not very good at telling yarns, for the boy is still the same with his innate hunger for romance, his readiness for imaginative adventure and his capacity for fun. Even today, with television invading every home and comics providing a weekly fare of juvenile purple pills, the appeal of live story-telling cannot be replaced by any mechanical means, and is one of the greatest educational mediums. Few parents nowadays tell their children stories or introduce them to the delights of children's literature.

I remember giving a new boy a little talk about his Promise and when I asked if he had any questions he said: "Please, can you explain how a jet plane works?" I know now that a boy has a built-in defence mechanism against "little talks". It would have been much more effective if I had told him a story about flying, mentioning in the course of the excitement that the Pilot had prayed for help, and that he was doing his best to serve his Queen.

Yarning, acting, making things, achieving small skills, getting out to find out and explore, these things must never be omitted from the Cub Programme and must always be geared to fun: fun alike in games and in work, fun in belonging to a gang with secret signs and symbolism; super fun just being a Cub.

There is a peculiar magic in Cubbing which must never be impaired.

SCOUTING PROVERBS

1 Look with the eyes of the boy.
2 Those who never make mistakes never make Patrol Leaders.
3 A boy's memory is as long as a guinea-pig's tail.
4 It isn't the problem boy that produces the problem Troop; it's the problem Scouter.
5 If boys imitate us, and they do, then some of their faults might be ours as well.
6 It is better to blow out the match than to burn down the city.
7 Physical toughness is a good servant but a bad master: the thugs and barbarians throughout history have been physically tough.
8 Stern words are like coins, the more there are the lower their value.
9 Empty Scouters make the most noise—especially at committee meetings.
10 Behind the action lies the motive; behind the motive the man.
11 A Scout's duty is to help others—even if the others are members of the same Group Council.
12 It's a poor Scout who does nothing but Scouting.
13 Don't put on an act—boys are shrewd dramatic critics.
14 A boy joins the Scouts because he likes it, and leaves the Scouts because he no longer likes it. It's as simple as that.
15 You can be a mirror in which the boy sees reflected the man he would like to be—or you can be a glass he can see through.
16 Boy differs from boy. Why then expect them all to go the same place? Why try and pour them into the same mould?
17 A friendly frown is better than a foolish smile.
18 An aim cannot be achieved if you are not clear what the aim is.
19 All play and no work does not make Jack a Scout.
20 The Programme should be devised for the boy not the boy forced to fit the programme.
21 Beware of uniformity.

SCOUTING
AND THE PUBLIC

I

Sixty years ago there suddenly appeared in our villages, towns and cities boys dressed in the strange garb of cowboy hats, neckerchiefs, shirts decorated with some bright ribbons on the left shoulders, and, particularly unusual in those days of knickerbockers, short trousers; and they would be armed with broomsticks! For all to see, the Boy Scouts had arrived and no doubt it was the first the majority of the astonished citizens of our land had heard of *Scouting for Boys*. But it would not be the last! Before long many of them would have been the recipients of acts of kindness those boys called their daily Good Turn. Undoubtedly, in those early days, as in the days and years to follow, the obligation and willingness to serve their fellow men without reward made a profound impression. The phrase "the Good Turn" became part of our language overnight.

This attitude of mind to serve, inculcated by

the Scout Promise "to help other people at all times" and implicit in the motto "Be Prepared", had its first spectacular test with the outbreak of War in 1914. Baden-Powell issued what he termed a Mobilisation Order and some of the tasks he offered his Scouts were guarding and patrolling bridges, culverts, telegraph lines, etc., against spies; collecting information as to supplies and transport available; distributing notes to householders and other duties connected with billeting, commandeering and warning; relief measures; messenger work; helping with the sick and wounded; and acting as guides and orderlies. These duties and many more were undertaken.

Three days after the declaration of war, for instance, the Admiralty asked for a thousand Sea Scouts to undertake coast-watching work on the East Coast. This essential service continued until the end of the War and there was no shortage of volunteers when replacements were needed as the Scouts reached the age for duty with the Armed Forces. Over twenty thousand Sea Scouts were employed as coast-watchers between August 1914 and November 1918. In the early days most Scout Troops could boast at least one bugle and many boasted several among their prized possessions so that people living near their meeting places were often, to put it mildly, exasperated by so-called bugle practices which were of varying degrees of proficiency. But the neighbours' exasperation quickly changed to gratitude which was felt by the public generally when Scout buglers undertook the task of sounding the "All Clear" after air-raids. That these Scouts of fifty years ago met the challenge there is not a shadow of doubt. B.-P.'s expectations were more than realised and the Movement had earned the admiration and goodwill of the general public.

Service to the public was not, and is not, of course, confined to periods of national emergency. In good times and bad, Scouts are "prepared" to give a hand when called on or when they see a need. An example of the latter comes to mind. During the economic depression between the Wars, the Movement both nationally and locally organised, with considerable success, a number of schemes for training the unemployed in new skills and for occupying the time of the unemployed in useful pursuits. Another well worth while undertaking during these difficult times was the adoption of the Durham town of Tow Law by the Rover Scouts of London.

The beginning of the trail: "On my honour I promise to do
my duty . . ."

Adventurous activities lie at the heart of Scouting: gliding, sailing, cooking for example but so do the outdoor life and the call of the far horizon and "laughter and the love of friends", and all these things come together around the Camp Fire: "As the flames point upward, so be our aim . . ."

The height of a Scout's achievement: to become a Queen's Scout

II

Since the Royal Charter of Incorporation was granted in 1912, the Sovereign had been Patron of The Association. It was a great pleasure, therefore, to be invited by the newly instituted King George's Jubilee Trust to assist in the sale of the official souvenir programme on the occasion of the Silver Jubilee of King George V and Queen Mary on 6th May, 1935. The Scouts of London were responsible for sales along the royal route from Buckingham Palace to St. Paul's Cathedral while in other parts of the country the Scouts sold programmes at local celebrations of the occasion. The Movement's own celebration was the building and lighting a chain of 1,775 beacons throughout the United Kingdom at 10 p.m. on Jubilee Day. Two years later, almost to the day, the Movement was privileged to assist at another royal occasion— the Coronation of King George VI on 12th May, 1937. Again, King George's Jubilee Trust sought the help of Scouts in the sale of the souvenir programme along the royal route, and in every part of the Commonwealth. Nearly 600,000 copies were sold in the United Kingdom alone. In addition, 1,650 London Rover Scouts assisted the Police by erecting, manning throughout the great day and dismantling 2,400 crush barriers along the Coronation route. Another 125 Rover Scouts were on duty outside Westminster Abbey helping with the guests' cars and messengers. B.-P. wrote afterwards: "Everyone I spoke to was impressed by the businesslike way in which they (the Scouts) applied themselves to the various jobs for which they were detailed, and I heard it frequently said that the boys of this Association, more than any other, seem to know what to do on these occasions."

At this time, the situation in Europe was uneasy, to say the least, and the Movement's participation in the joyous events just recalled did not prevent it from looking ahead. Scouting must continue to "Be Prepared" for any eventuality and so, in 1937, B.-P. wrote to the Home Secretary offering the services of Scouts and Rover Scouts in connection with Air Raid Precautions. The offer gratefully accepted, encouragement was given to Scouts to qualify for the Ambulance, Pathfinder and Signaller badges and for everyone over fourteen years of age to co-operate in local arrangements. B.-P. wrote at the time: We shall not precipitate

War by being prepared." The Movement's preparedness had its test during the national emergency of the following year. Where weaknesses were discovered steps were taken to eliminate them and a National Service Badge for everyone over 14 years of age was introduced. The requirements included verbal message-carrying, reporting, knowledge of the locality, fitting and care of civilian gas-masks, the preservation of discipline and an under-taking to render service in an emergency. Additionally, more training was encouraged in badges such as the Clerk, Cook, Cyclist and Fireman. This training proved to be of immense value when the call came in September, 1939. Again, the Scouts were prepared! And there was no lack of calls. Before hostilities began Scouts were already helping with evacuees, at Air Raid Precaution posts and in countless other ways. As the war took its course a variety of demands were made on the Movement. For assistance, within the first month there was an urgent appeal from the Paper Control Board for Scouts to help with the collection of waste-paper and a national scheme was put into operation within days. The Admiralty asked for Scout signallers to train for duty with merchant shipping convoys. Then there were the indoor air-raid shelters. The Minister of Home Security requested the Move-ment to undertake to assemble them in the homes of old people and where the men were away on war service. Teams of Scouts accepted the task—described by one of them as "a man's size Meccano"—with enthusiasm. Thousands of these shelters were built by Scouts and many householders who knew little or noth-ing of Scouting began to understand.

In 1943 Rover Scouts and Scouters were asked to send in their names if they were prepared to offer their services for relief work in due time among civilians in the liberated countries. Volunteers were forthcoming but how was it to be paid for—would the Movement help? Of course, it would; in one day of work it earned £33,000! Thus were the 97 members of the Scout International Relief Scheme enabled to give devoted service to their fellow men in sixteen countries. These activities are but a few of hundreds tackled during those grim years.

In 1947 the Movement was honoured to assist on the occasion of the wedding of our Queen—then Her Royal Highness The Princess Elizabeth—to Prince Philip. Twenty-six King's Scouts were on duty inside Westminster Abbey and forty Rover Scouts

assisted the Police outside it; one thousand Scouts sold programmes along the processional route—they sold out two hours
before the procession began!; and another party of King's Scouts
helped at the display of wedding presents. The following year
brought a request for help from the organisers of the 14th
Olympiad. At the athletics at Wembley sixty Scouts were on duty
as messengers each day; another sixty carried the name boards for
the competing countries; one hundred and eighty Scouts released
167,000 pigeons during the opening ceremony; others marked
out the Marathon course and helped in various ways. At Torbay,
where the yachting events took place, 200 Senior Scouts did yeo-
man work as markers, flag-bearers and parade leaders; they
ferried competitors and their gear; rigged and launched the Fire-
flies; and acted as messengers, despatch riders and interpreters.
One grateful official referred to them as "the oil within the wheels
of the Olympic organisation". On 3rd June, 1953, our Queen, the
Patron of our Association, was crowned in Westminster Abbey.
Needless to say, Scouts were again on duty. Before Coronation
Day, a messenger service was working at the Lord Chamber-
lain's Office and at the hotels where Her Majesty's personal guests
were staying. On the day itself, Scouts were much in evidence.
Helping the Police in the Forecourt of Buckingham Palace, outside the Abbey and at their temporary canteens; helping the news-
reel cameramen; helping those concerned with the official film
A Queen is Crowned; and helping the Jubilee Trust with the sale
of the souvenir programme. Four thousand Scouts and Scouters
were concerned with the latter task. The Movement found time
for its own celebrations, too. At 10 o'clock on Coronation Night
a chain of 1,390 beacons was lit throughout the United Kingdom
making a thrilling climax to a memorable day. In passing, it
should be mentioned, that for many years, Scouts have been
privileged to assist at Royal Garden Parties and on other occasions
at Buckingham Palace.

III

In 1948, the central organisation of the Movement was faced
with a financial crisis. Not for the first time nor, probably, the
last! But bearing in mind the economic state of the country and

the need for the Movement to develop its activities, it became clear that new sources of income must be found. In considering the problem, the Committee of the Council of The Association remembered the successful Days of Work in 1914 for the Pearson Fresh Air Fund and in 1944 for the Scout International Relief Scheme and it was suggested that, annually, every Scout should do a job for his Movement. And so came Bob-a-job; the annual effort when Scouts, for one week only, work for reward. Any doubts about its acceptance by the Movement and the public were quickly dispelled and the first Bob-a-Job Week—Easter week, 1949—was an unbounded success as have been the Weeks ever since. Not only do they provide essential funds for Scouting but the practical example of self-help has a big public appeal. It is as well that it has as, without the public's good will, there would be few jobs! The Movement owes a tremendous debt to the community for supporting Bob-a-Job so splendidly.

IV

But I would like to return for a moment to the early days. Before the Movement was two years old, B.-P. decided the time had come for Scouts from different parts of the country to meet and to give the public the opportunity of seeing for themselves that there were more Scouts than the local Patrol or Troop. Eleven thousand excited boys accepted their Chief's invitation and were present at this first big Scout Rally which was held on 4th September, 1909, at the Crystal Palace. A month later B.-P. held another Rally, in Glasgow, when 6,000 Scouts gathered from all parts of Scotland.

Probably, the most significant of those early Rallies was, however, that held at Windsor on 4th July, 1911, to mark the Coronation of King George V. Twenty-six thousand Scouts were there, on a very hot day, to see their new King and to be inspected by him. The King's manifestation of his approval of the Movement was not lost on the public at large.

A Rally with a difference took place in Birmingham in July, 1913. Not only were the public able to see Scouts in the mass— 18,000 of them on this occasion—but there was an exhibition of Scout skills for their interest and education. At the stalls, they could see at work Scout basket-makers, carpenters, electricians, engineers, farmers, handymen, plumbers, printers, shoe repairers and tailors; while in the arena there were displays of folk dancing and singing, pioneering, cycling, boxing, wrestling, gymnastics and lassooing. Another innovation was the presence of Scouts from Austria, Belgium, France, Germany, Italy, Spain, Sweden and the United States.

There were many other rallies (notably that phenomenal assembly at the Alexandra Palace on 7th October, 1922, when 20,000 Wolf Cubs, 43,000 Scouts and 2,000 Rover Scouts from all parts of the United Kingdom travelled to London *for the day* to form a Posse of Welcome to the Prince of Wales after his world tour), all important and picturesque in their day but by 1920 the rally was reserved largely for Counties and Districts and a new gathering came into being: the Jamboree.

V

The first Jamboree took the form of a camp in the Old Deer Park at Richmond and an exhibition and displays at Olympia. Five thousand Scouts from twenty-six parts of the world attended it and it lasted for ten days. The exhibition, while reminiscent of Birmingham seven years earlier, included a small zoo, a model colliery, a rifle range and a tracking ground where the public were invited to test their power of observation and deduction. Undoubtedly, the event was a great success from both the public and Scout points of view but valuable lessons were learned. The most important being that a Jamboree cannot be completely successful when those taking part are camping some miles away from the place in which they are to spend their waking hours. There were those, too, who felt that the exhibition, display and competition aspects of the venture had been overdone. So that when the next World Jamboree was held at Ermelunden in Denmark, four years later, the arrangements were very different. Everything took place in camp; religious services, displays, competitions and, of the greatest importance bearing in mind B.-P.'s concept of these gatherings, making friends. Only one innovation did not survive—the World Championship in Scout skills. Apart from this,

Denmark set the pattern for future world Jamborees—of which up to and including 1967 there have now been twelve.

In 1957 the Movement celebrated the Centenary of B.-P.'s birth and the Jubilee of Scouting. And what a wonderful year it was. Thanksgiving services in B.-P.'s old school, Charterhouse, and in Westminster Abbey; Glasgow's magnificent exhibition in the Kelvin Hall; a Troop and Patrol Leaders' Camp at Gilwell Park; and celebrations in village, town, city, county and country. The culmination of these rejoicings was an additional World Jamboree, a World Rover Moot and a World Scouters Indaba, held concurrently in Sutton Park, near Birmingham, from 1st–12th August. Thirty-five thousand Scouts, Rover Scouts and Scouters came from eighty-two parts of the world. The camp programme followed the familiar pattern for Jamborees and every participant took part in at least one day's excursion to places of interest in the Midlands where local Scouts acted as hosts. In addition, all of the visitors from overseas were offered hospitality in Scout homes before or after the event.

VI

To turn to an altogether different kind of public appearance! Soon after the Coming-of-Age Jamboree in 1929, the Rover Scouts of Holborn staged a revue they called *Good Turns*, written and produced by "A Holborn Rover". The following two years saw similar productions and by the third year the shows had earned a considerable reputation. One of their most enthusiastic supporters was the then County Commissioner for London, and in the Spring of 1932, he suggested to "A Holborn Rover" and the stage manager of the revues that something similar but on a larger scale, might be staged in a West End theatre under the auspices of the London Scout Council. In that meeting that phenomenon of Scout entertainment the *Gang Shows* was conceived and in October, 1932, the first All-London Scout Revue, consisting in the main of big musical ensembles and sketches—all written, composed and produced by "A Holborn Rover" (later to be revealed as Mr. Ralph Reader, as is now well known) with the title *The Gang's All Here!*, was staged. After a run of 3 days the theatre was booked for a week in 1933. To everyone's astonishment, every seat was sold before the opening performance. In 1934 the theatre was booked for a fortnight; the same thing happened, not a ticket left by the time the curtain went up on the first night, and so it has gone on ever since. *Gang Shows* were now an established part of the Scout scene, Scouts outside London began to stage their *Gang Shows;* Stoke-on-Trent was the first, then Glasgow, Newcastle-on-Tyne, Manchester, all using material from the London Show but with local Scout performers. To-day Gang Shows are staged by Groups, Districts and Counties in the United Kindom and in many parts of the Commonwealth. Additionally, a television version is screened annually and in 1964 TAM ratings estimated that it was seen in over seven million homes. In 1936 Ralph Reader broke new ground with a musical pageant play, *Boy Scout*, in the Royal Albert Hall. It had a cast of twelve hundred and a choir of 250 and was a splendid and moving spectacle. The play has been revived at intervals, the most recent presentation being in 1959.

VII

From the earliest days, B.-P. asked Scouts to re-affirm their Promise annually during the feast of their Patron Saint, St. George, and early in the nineteen-thirties it was felt that more emphasis might be given to this by holding a central Service for a few representatives from every County. Accordingly, arrangements were made with the Dean and Chapter of St. George's Chapel, Windsor Castle, for a Service to held there for King's Scouts and holders of Scout Gallantry Awards on the Sunday nearest St. George's Day and, afterwards, for the congregation to gather in the Horseshoe Cloister to salute the flag of St. George and to hear a short address by the Chief Scout. When the details had been settled for the first Service—which was held on 22nd April, 1934—King George V heard of them and, as he expected to be in residence at Windsor Castle at the time, expressed a desire to see the Scouts on their way to the Chapel. Since then, those taking part in the Service have always had the privilege of marching through the Quadrangle on their way to the Chapel and on many occasions the Scouts have been honoured by the Sovereign or another member of the Royal Family being present. Thanks to the B.B.C., the parade has been televised on a number of occasions. We continue to hope that one day viewers may be able to see the Service as well.

VIII

Much has, of necessity, been left out of this review of Scouting's links with our fellow countrymen who are not closely associated with the Movement. For instance, the acts of gallantry by Scouts; since the Movement began, 5,490 awards have been made for such service, frequently involving risk of life; for in this way, perhaps the most important way of all, Scouts met the public. Then there are the wide games; the camps in local parks; the service to old people and hospitals; the county and district rallies; and, maybe of greatest significance, the Scout on his way to and from his meetings. The cheerful, smart, helpful Scout has always been Scouting's most effective ambassador. May he ever be so!

SCOUTING PROVERBS

22 *Most bigheads have small minds.*

23 *Bad camping drives out good.*

24 *Kit expands to fit the rucsac available.*

25 *A Troop camps on its stomach.*

26 *Remember the boys you lost as well as the boys you kept.*

27 *One pat on the back is worth six kicks in the pants.*

28 *Never put yourself into a position from which there is no retreat.*

29 *The more you look back the more you move forward.*

30 *A good teacher strikes oil without boring.*

31 *If at first you don't succeed—you're normal.*

32 *You can't plough a field by turning it over in your mind.*

33 *We know where we are going, but a boy often shows us the way.*

34 *Do not choose to be wrong for the sake of being different.*

35 *It is only by doing things that you find out what you can do.*

36 *The art of living is the art of using experience—your own and other people's!*

37 *Never take disciplinary action until you have realised where you are going to be after you have taken it.*

38 *It is no good trying to force a boy from his mother's apron strings if you merely tie him to your own belt.*

39 *Every Scouter gets the Troop he deserves: the reverse unfortunately isn't always true.*

40 *When the Devil whispers to you "What a good Scouter you are!" pray quickly.*

41 *It's no use knowing something backwards if you don't go forward.*

42 *A boy is only a boy once, and a summer's opportunities missed is a summer gone for ever.*

SCOUTS IN SPITE OF EVERYTHING
—THE HANDICAPPED

How is it that the Scout Movement, which was created for boys, albeit without any stipulation that they should be ordinary boys, should appeal to those who are handicapped in some way such as necessitates some difference in the method of their education, which according to the degree of disability is often received in Special schools?

Surely, it is an inherent desire to do things and have fun, the sort of fun that Scouting provides and even though handicapped boys are more different to each other than are ordinary boys there is the desire for them to do things that other boys do and to belong to the same Body that provides the means for just this.

Although a Branch of the Movement for Disabled Scouts (as it was first known) was formed in 1926, handicapped boys had already found their way into Scouting, helped by the precepts laid down in the Scout Law. The title of the Branch was changed to "Special Tests" in 1928 and again in 1936 when the present title of Handicapped Scout Branch was adopted.

Fundamentally, the object of the Branch was to give specialist help and develop Scouting among boys with a physical or mental handicap. It was a challenge that was quickly taken up and soon there were Troops in Orthopedic hospitals, Sanatoria and Special schools also in hospitals for the mentally sub-normal.

Many boys who have some physical handicap have shown that they do really want to be boys—in spite of everything and Scouting can and does help them to achieve this.

B-P in his book *Life's Snags*, as a prefix to the Chapter entitled "The Will's the Thing", wrote "To do anything in life you must have will-power—or you won't get there". There have been many examples of achievement over adversity shown by Scouts who are handicapped and although Scouting's highest award for Courage, the Cornwell Badge, was not created specifically for them but for all members of the Movement, there are many examples on record of courage and fortitude shown by handicapped Scouts.

One example concerns a boy who was born without ears. He was a Cub in a London Group and during his stay in hospital where he was receiving plastic surgical operations to make "ears" from skin taken from his biceps, he continued his Scouting. The Hospital Surgeon recommended that the Cub's fortitude was of a very high order and worthy of an award.

A visit to the boy's home to follow up this independent recommendation revealed that now he had received "ears" from the Surgeon, he would like to learn to play the violin, Yehudi Menuhin being his inspiration. He duly qualified for the Musician's Badge, and undoubtedly his association with other Scouts who "accepted" him helped to dissolve his consciousness of his deformed "ears". As B-P said—"The Will's the Thing".

Challenge and Achievement are correlative to Scouting and are recognised by handicapped boys as the Scouting programme progressively unfurls for them. It has been said that insufficient has been published of the work of the Handicapped Scout Branch and of the achievements of Scouts who are handicapped. The achievements may be seen and indeed are seen by the few who are working closest with the handicapped and, rather naturally, little fuss is made of the "combined operation".

Of course, the proper encouragement of parents is very important to a handicapped boy, and as an example of a "combined operation", and there are many to be found in this Branch of Scouting. Here, in my opinion, is an inspiring story.

"My dad's like me!" This was the greeting by a Scout to a Scoutmaster. It was apparent from the squeaks accompanying his rather cumbersome gait, that he was wearing artificial legs. The

Scout handshake showed further, in passing, that he had but stumps with tiny "fingers" in substitution for hands. When the meaning of the definite introduction had manifested itself, it was apparent that he was proud of his dad, who was similarly handicapped. The preliminaries over, the Scout (a member of a normal Group) explained that he was very keen to become a Queen Scout. Could he? he asked. The programme of qualifying tests was checked and he knew what he had to do and that where necessary, there might be some substitution of an alternative for the normal test where this might be detrimental to his physical powers. In any alternative test there would be required the same degree of personal effort and similar objective. His next test was to be swimming as a qualification for the First Class Badge. At the bath-edge, he was some fifteen inches shorter as he stood without his artificial legs, balancing on his stumps. This was a "success" story, no announcements—just a Boy Scout swimming without much leg-help and no hands to paddle the water—but with will-power, patience, and achievement as his reward.

Because of ever-increasing medical skills and the increased care of the very young, there are certainly fewer long-term child patients in Orthopedic hospitals, which is reflected in there being fewer hospital-sponsored Scout Groups. Nevertheless, the 1964 census of the Movement showed that there were 4,624 handicapped Scouts in the United Kingdom; an increase of approximately 300 over the year 1962. There are, however, many boys with minor handicaps, who although helped by Scouting are not recorded and rightly so.

Today, a handicapped boy living at home may belong to an ordinary Scout Group, where he will receive his training along side non-handicapped boys thus helping to equip himself to be able to take his place in due course, as an adult in a normal adult world. The practice of integrating handicapped boys with non-handicapped boys in Scouting offers a two-way benefit to both, for "children that are handicapped are just children, and handicapped Scouts are just Scouts".

The Ministry of Education (England and Wales) have established seven categories into which handicapped children may be placed; Blind, Partially Sighted, Deaf, Partially Hearing, Blind and Deaf, Physically Handicapped, Delicate (including Diabetics), also Educationally Sub-normal.

Boys with these handicaps are eligible to become Scouts and enjoy the companionship of other boys. All Scouts are required to make the same Promise and, whether handicapped or not, they comply, with the same minimum conditions of membership, voluntarily and without reservations.

Under the Ministry category of Physically Handicapped, we have in Scouting boys who are handicapped through Muscular Dystrophy, Cerebral Palsy, Poliomylitis, Spina Bifida, Results of Accidents and Malformations such as are caused by Thalidomide.

Although Scouting is not concerned with active medical treatment of handicapped boys, specialist training courses are available for Scouters having handicapped boys in their Groups, so that they will understand the general aspects of the different types of handicap, limitations in movement and the requirements for personal comfort whilst they are in their care.

In 1949 the Scout Associations of Holland arranged an International camp for handicapped Scouts, which was called an "Agoon". The word "Agoon" is derived from the Greek word Agou meaning a Meeting or Competition, and by its use as the name of a Camp, the functional title of "Handicapped" can be dispensed with, with advantage to the feelings of the Scouts.

Of course, the journey to a country overseas can be tiring, and a lot of extra arrangements have to be made, for nothing can be left to chance. But I am sure that such expeditions are of value and worthwhile.

On the way home from Ommen in the East of Holland, the U.K. party halted for refreshments at the Café on the great Dyke separating the North Sea from the Ijselmeer. One Scout, with a caliper splint on each leg saw a challenge in the climb up the steep slope of grass bank of the Dyke, leading to the Café. Ignoring the steps and throwing down his crutches he made a dash for the summit, which he reached proudly, yelling for all to hear that he had conquered Everest! "Joie de Vivre" indeed!

A further "Agoon" was held in Belgium in 1953, and another in England, at Gilwell Park in 1958.

At home, specially planned camps known as "Agoonorees" are held each year at which the more severely handicapped are able to take an active part together with non-handicapped Scouts. Working under the Patrol system, a varied and progressive active programme of training is carried out.

In addition to the usual provisions made for a Troop camp, there is a service staff including a resident Medical officer, a qualified nursing staff and a small team of "Den Mothers", all of whom are Scouters. The "Den Mothers" help to care for incontinent boys who are thus able to participate in Scouting's peak activity involving all the fun of cooking in the open air, bridge-building, swimming (where permitted), sports, Camp-Fires and the companionship of many others, and often far from home.

These camps provide indelible memories for the remainder of each year and successively build up a sense of achievement in the lives of all campers, and a feeling of purpose and belonging, as in other children.

And this one or two weeks' period of an "Agoonoree" each year, when their sons are in our care, often enables the parents to take a well-earned rest and holiday, thus providing for the Scouts of the "Agoonoree" a latent but realistic additional daily good turn.

The number of handicapped in camp varies according to the Region. The London "Agoonoree" comprises between 60 to 80 with an additional 100 or so non-handicapped Scouts, Rovers and Scouters. Some thirty wheel-chairs add to the responsibilities of the camp staff and an unusual item of camp equipment consists of a comprehensive tool-box for the repair and maintenance of the wheel-chairs, caliper-splints and artificial limbs, under the charge of an engineer-Scouter. It is surprising how quickly wheel-chairs etc. need remedial attention when subjected to camp usage.

Wherever there is a Scout Group there is the possibility for a handicapped boy or two becoming members. Specialist Commissioners in each County are anxious to help Group Scouters to understand the problems of the handicapped boy so that his integration into Scouting will be without detriment to the programme for the rest of the Group.

Basically it is important to concentrate on what a boy *can* do, rather than what he cannot, and an initial simple explanation to the boy's parents and then to the Cub Pack or to the Scout Troop will give the "combined operation" a good foundation.

A handicapped boy knows his limitations so far as activities are concerned and will not expect to join in the more boisterous games or type of activity needing physical stamina. But as a member of the unit, having prepared and trained with the rest, he will follow every step of a practical project with a sense of participation acquired during the planning stage, as for instance in a pioneering project.

To be really effective and enjoyable, Scouting for the handicapped must be the real thing, not a watered-down version, but having an application adjusted where necessary to enable a boy to take part in spite of . . . everything.

Development of Scouting with the handicapped must follow as closely as possible to the normal pattern, and whatever developments may be planned in the future, the imagination, ingenuity and patience and dedication of the Scouters serving through the Handicapped Branch will make this possible.

The spiritual aspect of Scouting . . . Belief in God . . . will surely be the "Staff and Comforter" to those who through Scouting have something real to give to the handicapped, something that will help them to a purposeful life.

Encouragement, if it is needed, will be found through contact with the handicapped, particularly, I feel sure, those who are Scouts in spite of everything.

This citation written by a Doctor in support of an application for a Scout Cornwell award surely confirms the challenge:

"Besides any physical suffering he may have endured, he has had a great mental suffering in his desire to be as other children and in his hope that he, too, might one day participate in all their normal pursuits."

BIG BUSINESS

Scouting today is not only the country's (the world's?) leading Youth Movement; it is big business!

For consider: at the last (1965) census there were (in round figures, to make calculation easy!) some 236,000 Wolf Cubs. To provide a Wolf Cub with jersey, cap, scarf, woggle, shorts, socks, costs about £2 12s 0d. So that if all the Wolf Cubs were wearing uniforms at the same time (as they probably were on the occasion of their Golden Jubilee National Pack Meeting in June, 1966) they would be wearing £613,600 worth of uniform—not counting the badges!

Or take the Scouts: at the last census there were roughly 228,600 Scouts between 12 and 18 and their uniform costs something between three and four pounds according to quality, say £3 10s. So if all the Scouts, etc., etc. they would be wearing no less than £800,000 worth of uniform, again not counting the badges!

There are also Scouters and Commissioners but no doubt you've got the point about uniform. But there are other things—Headquarters for instance. There are over 12,000 Groups in the United Kingdom and how many have their own H.Q. is not accurately known but suppose it's, at a low estimate, a quarter, and suppose the average value is £2,000 which is probably ludicrous, but it represents £6,000,000! And all the Groups have equipment of some sort—tents, rope, camp cooking equipment, sisal, axes, dining shelters . . . Suppose there are three Patrols per Troop and each Patrol has its tent, which may cost anything from say £21 to £31 each—which makes at an average of £26, some £936,000 worth of tents in use if all the Patrols were camping. A Gilwell hand axe costs a pound: every Patrol needs one at least; surely a third of all Scouts have rucsacs?—they cost between £4 and £7 each. Sleeping bags? about the same price and about the same number of boys in them, I suppose. It all adds up to a lot of money . . .

There are people: for every Cub or Scout in the Movement there are probably at least five adults counting parents, neighbours, relatives, friends actively interested in him in his uniformed capacity—which makes two and a half million at any one time.

There are 12 H.Q. Camp Sites: their total average is 109 acres and Gilwell has another 108 acres. There are many, many district-owned and county-owned sites too; the total acreage of these is unknown but added up they would surely make a small county.

There are books: during the last complete year the three leading Scout book publishers, Messrs. Pearsons, Messrs. Brown, Son and Ferguson and we ourselves sold, in round figures, some 608,000 books.

And this is just our *Scouting.*

Now the last census gave our World figures as 10,350,540 . . .

"Cancelled? Why??"

A THANK YOU TO
OUR FRIENDS...

1 *To Parents*

Although of course all parents in our eyes are equal some are more equal than others. There are (regretfully) the utterly indifferent—who are equally indifferent no doubt about their son's life in any context—but there aren't in our experience many of them; there are the lukewarm; and the deeply involved. (There is a small sub-class in the latter category which might be labelled the over enthusiastic but this is a small burden for us to bear compared to the dead inertia of those who do not care, or who care but little.)

Many of you care very much and you are the golden hearts whom here we salute and thank for your support and trust over sixty years.

There isn't much to which you cannot and do not turn your hand. It is you who attend the Troop Open Night and the "Troop Show" nights (for which you also play the piano, make the costumes and make-up the cast); it is you who burn petrol on journeys short and long in all kinds of weather for some Scout reason or other; it is you who put up the bazaar stalls and run the jumble sales. The Group Committee relies on you for most of its members: you are secretaries, treasurers, chairmen, Group Quartermasters, Bob-a-Job organisers ... You have been known not only to raise the funds to build a Group H.Q. (that lovely ambition of any Group to have a place of its own) but through long summer and cold winter have actually built it, brick by brick, and plank by plank.

Most important of all see that your sons fulfil their obligations of Patrol Nights, Troop Nights and Camps and encourage them on their journey through First Class to the Queen's Scout Badge. For we as Scouters must never forget we are *your* Scouters, in *your* Group serving *your* sons (and for entrusting them to us, allowing us to share in the great task of leading them to manhood, we thank you. We do it because we like doing it: but we couldn't do it if you didn't let us).

So it is you, dear parents, who entrust him to the wide meadows and dark woods of his first camp—a theme on which not long ago Ann Tudor wrote these words:

> *There's a polished gleam in the hall tonight*
> *No muddy marks, or leaves, or crumbs;*
> *A shiny knocker, the door knob bright,*
> *No sign of wet or sticky thumbs.*
>
> *And there's not an odd sock on the bathroom floor;*
> *The bedspread has never a crease or book;*
> *But a very brief postcard has come to the door—*
> *"Dear Mum, swell time, but wish you were cook!"*
>
> *There's a breathless quiet in the house tonight—*
> *No homework sighs, no radio fun;*
> *No clump of boots upon the stairs;*
> *No off-key songs, no taps let run.*
>
> *And there's never a sound of whistling shrill,*
> *Or a screech of "Where shall I find it Mum?"*
> *House beautiful and clean,*
> *House empty and mean.*
> *Oh hurry back from camp, my son.*

Later his First Class Journey will be fun to be enjoyed— or usually is if he is properly prepared and his Scouters know their job. But listening to the rain lashing down and watching the mist on the hills, to you it will always be an ordeal to be endured. As one mother wrote:

> *He ventured forth, complete with stave and pack,*
> *And grim determination on his face,*
> *Armed with a map and compass, nothing more,*
> *Given one short day in which to reach a place*
> *Appointed by the powers that be; my heart*
> *Was heavy as I watched him go . . .*

But your restraint brings its reward:

> *. . . when, late the following day*
> *I heard his cheery voice and saw his face.*
> *Badly fatigued his body may have been,*
> *But in his bearing was a new found grace.*
> *Shyly but happily, with halting voice,*
> *The tale was told, right to the journey's end.*

Reward indeed! So you as parents please support your Scouters as far as you can or farther:

> *they win no wars who peep at life askance*
> *and shoot wise saws from sheltered ignorance.*

We offer your boy adventure and excitement as well as friendship and faith. Support your sons: support your Scouters. And turn up when a chance is offered you—to the Group's A.G.M., to the Summer Camp Report Meeting (if there is one), to open nights of Pack or Troop, to the Group Annual Dinner. Take your fair share in the fund-raising efforts. Play your part in this great game. And today as never before we have need of real experts (of necessity a Scouter's expertise is spread thinly over many subjects like a little butter in a large slice of toast): and every dad is an expert in *something*. What is more, many are old Scouts. The outstanding need of any Scoutmaster several times a year (or several times a month!) is for badge testers: boys hate waiting. A Scouter in time saves nine and any Dad with the not very recondite knowledge or experience could become just for an hour or

two "a temporary Scouter". We repeat: no Scouter can be an
expert in the whole of modern Scouting; its not his job to be. It
is his job to know where the experts are to be found and here too
you can help him by finding him them.

You cannot live your sons' lives for them: neither can we. But
together we can help him to live it. A few months ago, our
Chief Scout said:"We are in business, big business and we work
with the most precious material in the world, God's children."
God's children—and your sons: thank you Mums and Dads.
Thank you, partners!

2   *To Scouters' Wives*

"It's your birthday, dear", says the Scouter in the cartoon to his
wife "what do you want to do?—go to the theatre or the Camp
Fire at the 7th?"

A few years ago in *The Scouter*, too, there appeared a very
popular series of cartoons called "Why Scoutmasters' wives grow
weary". But dear wives, if sometimes you do grow a little weary
of the demands made upon you by your husband's enthusiastic
hobby of looking after other people's sons, most of the time you
give him your loyal support and understanding, and make sacri-
fices, as he does, of leisure hours, of peace of mind, even of money.
Because you know the fine work he is doing. It may be that, once
upon a time, you considered all Scouts and Scouters lunatics (and
indeed all good ones *are* a little crazy): but as you came to know
them more and more you realised that here were in a distraught
world happy groups of people and you were pleased when they
accepted you—sometimes when you were persuaded into uniform as completely one of them—and always as a friend. So we
thank you for everything; but especially:

For hours spent at home alone because of Troop Nights and
Pack Nights and committee meetings and Courts of Honour;

For holidays sacrificed to the demands of summer camps;

For forgiving the untidy gardens because there simply wasn't
time for Scouting *and* gardening;

For youthful muddy shoes on carpets understandingly for-
given;

For all those cups of tea and cakes provided generously at all
hours of day and night;

For sharing your home with so many small boys in peculiar caps, and with leggy Scouts and enthusiastically hearty adults in be-badged uniforms with a jargon of their own;

For all those shirts and shorts and scarves you pressed;

For all those things the Scouts "borrowed" and which somehow were never returned;

For letters written, accounts kept, calls made;

For endless hours spent at bazaars and jumble sales and Group shows;

For listening to problems which weren't yours, except that you made them so;

For, in short, understanding our dedication and forgiving it! Thank you, one and all.

3   *To Laymen in the Movement*

For bringing a leaven of common sense and sound judgement into what, without you, can become a slightly crazy society.

For bringing your talents to the common pool of skills.

For seeing the need of active help, and not mere passive approval.

For leaving firesides or gardens for interminable meetings on the hard seats of draughty schoolrooms and headquarters.

For sometimes suffering fools gladly—or at least for suffering fools.

For being let down yet coming back for more.

For creating good order and progress out of the chaos of the unbusinesslike.

For that abiding sense of humour that can turn tension into amity.

For a courteous hearing to what at times must seem outlandish plans.

For a contentment that the limelight should shine on others.

For the patient instruction of the apparently subnormal.

For laughing when you well might curse.

For all these things—our thanks.

Our thanks as well for wisdom and restraint in knowing when to help and when to leave alone, and knowledge when to speak and when to listen.

For serving and not directing.

For persuading and not dictating.

For conceding that you, as well as your Scouters, may be sometimes wrong.

For realising that there is not a "Scout side" or a "Lay side" but only one side—the Boys' side.

For being content that your Scouters may sometimes let you use the Headquarters built by your hands with the money you raised—when the boys can spare it.

For offering smiling congratulations to others who, with not one tenth of your record of service, receive Civic or National recognition.

For sitting cheerfully on the back row at the A.G.M. while they descend from the platform to have their photographs taken with the Mayor.

For watching the men with whom you work or play for signs of a potential Scouter or Instructor, and for passing on the good news.

For looking ever wider and scorning to build, within the framework of Scouting, a little empire of your own surrounded by little notices bearing the legend "No Interference. Keep Out".

For tact and patience and that greatest virtue, steadfastness.

For willingness to have a go at something that appals you and that you have never tried before.

For neglecting the attractive social occasion and accepting in its stead snow, fog, hail and cold discomfort, that a handful of boys somewhere may have better Scouting.

For keeping a corner of a busy life free in which to do something for nothing but the fun of doing it.

For accepting with a shrug the penalty of all who have ever truly blazed a trail.

Well I know who'll take the credit, all the clever chaps who followed,
Came a dozen men together, never knew my desert fears.
Tracked me by the camps I'd quitted, used the water holes I'd hollowed,
They'll go back and do the talking, they'll be called the pioneers.

Where you are numerous, there lies our strength.

Where you are scarce and hard to come by, there lies our weakness.

To a greater or lesser degree we have leaned on you for sixty years.

In the complicated world in which we live today, we cannot build the future without more and ever more of you woven into its fabric.

Thank you one and all!—and go on with us for another sixty years . . . At least!

4   *To all those other Friends . . .*

No man is an island and no Scout Group can be an island either: nor can the Scout Movement.

Nor has it.

We have been fortunate in our friends whom here, in our diamond year, we would especially remember and thank them for the goodwill they have shown us: in advice and in assistance in a thousand ways.

To you!—Education authorities, both National and Local, for lifting us over financial hurdles we could not surmount alone!

To you!—departments of Local Authorities: Policemen and Firemen, Baths attendants and attendants in Museums for placing your skilled knowledge at our disposal.

To you!—Voluntary Aid Societies and Sporting bodies!

To you National Trust, Nature Conservancy, National Parks Commission, the Forestry Commission, the Central Council of Physical Recreation and the Outward Bound Trust: especially for courses and camp sites and constant co-operation.

To you!—H.M.'s Royal Navy, H.M.'s Army, H.M.'s Royal Air Force for the spirit of brotherhood shown in so many practical ways.

To you Churches! For accepting us into the framework of your parish life and for the spirit of compromise which permits a full Scout programme without too much cavelling at weekend camps!

To you headmasters! for understanding about homework on Troop nights, for sponsoring so many fine Troops!

To you! Rotary Clubs and Round Tables living up to your motto of "Service above Self" meeting us half way for we are fellow travellers!

To you! Toc H. especially the one of you who said: "Service

is the rent we owe for our room on Earth," a reminder to us always.

To you the Press! to you the British Broadcasting Corporation, to you the Independent Television Authority!

> "Who write where many read, and speak where many listen"

and speak well of us, we pray you: for our cause is good and just.

And you!—the great Industrial Firms who increasingly lend your prestige and your power, and sponsor our undertakings.

To you B.-P. Guild! who, in addition to carrying the spirit of Scouting into the factories and offices of the land, are ever ready to put your shoulders to the wheel of any of our endeavours.

To you! vast multitude who support "Bob-a-Job" week by cheerfully finding jobs—and often making them—and suffering importunity with good grace: by rewarding generously.

No man is an island, and no man can stand alone: nor can we.

So, to all friends named above and any we may have failed to remember, for sixty years of understanding, assistance and encouragement: thank you very much.

THE COMMONWEALTH AND
HEADQUARTERS

There have been a Commonwealth Department and a Commonwealth Commissioner—under different names—at Headquarters almost as long as Scouting itself: as early as 1910 a Commissioner was appointed to encourage the development of Scouting in the British Empire, as it then was, and he himself was known as Commissioner for Colonies! Through the years the title of his office has moved by way of Commissioner for Overseas Dominions and Overseas Commissioner to its present Commonwealth Commissioner which not only sums up a lot of our history but indicates the way in which the department's responsibilities have changed.

The first members of the Commonwealth to have Scouts were Canada, Australia and New Zealand all in 1908 (B.-P. visited Canada in 1910 and Australia and New Zealand in 1912). In 1909 there was Scouting in British Guiana, India and Malta and by 1910 in Jamaica, Kenya, Malaya and Rhodesia. In the early days every Commonwealth Association was a branch of our own Boy Scout's Association. But as soon as it was possible according to their stage of development constitutions were granted to Branches to run their own Scouting and indeed Canada, Australia and New Zealand were very soon virtually self-governing, although in fact Canada did not become a member of the World Scout Conference (that is with no longer any official ties with our own H.Q.) until 1946 and the other two countries till 1953.

As commonwealth countries have moved rapidly towards independence in this last decade or so, it has been an important function of the Commonwealth Department (its most important function?) to help strengthen and develop the Scouting of the emergent nations so that their Scouting could stand strong and upright when the break came. Today (i.e. as I write in 1966) 35 Overseas Branches remain with a membership of some 55,000 but no doubt before long these, too, will become independent in their own right. But still today the department's function remains—to be "respon-sible to the Chief Scout and the Committee of the Council for the administration of Scouting in the Overseas Branches and to keep in close touch with the independent countries of the Commonwealth, acting as channel of communication between them and Scouting in this country."

The appointment of a Travelling Commissioner for overseas, invaluable in itself, has also of course been of great assistance to the department. The present holder of the appointment, George Witchell, who gave up the post of Training Secretary at Headquarters to undertake it writes for you now.

THE COMMONWEALTH
AND SCOUTING

WHEN Scouting was so enthusiastically received in the United Kingdom, it was inevitable that it should spread in the sphere of British influence, known then as the Empire and now the Commonwealth.

Even in 1908, the year *Scouting for Boys* was written, Scout Branches were registered in Australia, Canada and New Zealand, followed a year later by British Guiana, India (including the parts now Pakistan) and Malta. The next few years saw new Branches formed in quick succession, until every part of the Commonwealth, with the exception of the Falkland Islands and the Antarctic continent, had a recognised organisation to serve the boys who wanted to be Scouts.

The Movement in the Commonwealth started in many different ways. In some places, the missionaries, commercial representatives or government officials introduced the new idea. In others, overseas students in the U.K. became members and took home news about the Scouts, while in some cases, boys who could read English read a copy of *Scouting for Boys* and started in the same way as in the British Isles. In all these places, there was a demand from the boys themselves. The Movement was never organised until it already existed, and where it had grown naturally. It was nowhere forcibly introduced.

Because Scouting dealt with the fundamental needs of youth, it struck a responsive chord in youngsters of all races. The desire for responsibility, the challenge of adventure and service, the chance of proving manhood seem to be universal. It certainly caught the imagination of millions of boys, probably because it was exciting, new and progressive. Baden-Powell spent many years in Africa and Asia, and drew upon his experiences in many countries when he framed his training programme for youth. In fact, the ideas of Scouting are as much African and Asian as they are European.

When a country becomes independent, the Scout Movement in that country ceases to be a Branch, and becomes an independent Scout Association. In this way, Scouting keeps in step with political and administrative changes. The Boy Scouts Association headquarters in London are technically responsible for the Branches overseas, and are concerned with boys in such places as Gibraltar and the Solomon Islands as well as boys in Blackpool and Southend. This transition from a Branch to an independent Association is achieved smoothly and simply by giving progressively increasing responsibility and ensuring that, as well as having local leadership, the Scout Movement has its roots deep in the lives and hearts of the local community. Presidents, Prime Ministers, other Ministers, leaders in the fields of medicine, education and religion in some emergent Commonwealth countries, have been Scouts and Scouters, and are keen to encourage the progress and influence of Scout training which they know and understand.

Because of its flexible nature, Scouting can be moulded to suit local requirements of climate, religion, race, customs and national temperament, without losing any of the essential principles and aims. The needs of practical training differ a great deal and are changed to suit local conditions. Some Scout tests in the United Kingdom are obviously ridiculous in the tropics, such as learning how to rescue people who have fallen through the ice. The Scouts in the Gilbert and Ellice Islands, in the middle of the Pacific Ocean, do not have a badge for swimming, because any boy of four years of age could pass the Master Swimmer badge, and possibly could swim before he could walk. Such tests as "know what to do when seized by a crocodile", "demonstrate the correct treatment for snake-bite", and "cook ugali, meat and cabbage or make a chapatti and a curry" are sensible local variants.

Scouting is not only established in the main centres of population, but has spread to the most unlikely places. This is perhaps due to the fact that a great number of Scouts Groups are based on schools, because boys are found there in numbers, and many teachers have become Scoutmasters. With the spread of educational facilities, the Scout Movement has kept pace. As a result, Scouts can be found in the remote vastness of the Kalahari Desert, on lonely coral atolls in the middle of the Pacific Ocean, in longhouses of the Sea Dyaks in Sarawak, among the Esquimau people who live in Northern Canada, and in the Ruwenzori—the legendary Mountains of the Moon.

Within the Commonwealth, we can find flourishing Scout Groups among the Arab, African, Chinese, Malay, Melanesian, Polynesian, Micronesian, and Eskimo communities, as well as many others. Our members embrace nearly all the faiths in the world, including Buddhists, Muslims, Hindus, Jains, Sikhs, and Parsis, as well as most denominations of the Christian faith.

The enthusiasm for Scouting in many places is quite remarkable. In British Guiana, a Cub Pack and Scout Troop chiefly composed of Amerindians, paddled their canoes for 120 miles down the Mazaruni River to attend a one-day rally. Scouts in Papua chartered a boat, earning the money by diving for trochus shells and made a sea journey of 350 miles to attend a rally and meet the Chief Scout of the Commonwealth. At the same event, a Troop tacked for 80 miles against the wind in their outrigger canoes to attend. Three Masai Scoutmasters walked 200 miles to be present at a training course in Kenya. In the Solomon Islands, Scoutmasters have spent weeks travelling from isolated islands in order to be trained, and able to give better Scouting to the boys they lead. The great wave of enthusiasm is still active after sixty years.

Groups meet in a great variety of places. Some have built their own headquarters, ranging from permanent buildings costing thousands of pounds, to grass huts built in the school grounds. Many have open-air headquarters, being a plot of land with places cleared for each Patrol, often sown with flowering shrubs and kept neat and pleasant. In Hong Kong, where great resettlement blocks of flats have been built, the Scouts and Cubs meet on the flat roofs above their homes. In some places they have built a place of their own on stilts above the water. Many meet in the open air until the rainy season when they have to use school buildings. Groups are run in juvenile prisons, approved schools, hospitals, blind schools and in leper settlements. Wherever there is a demand for Scouting, and adequate leadership is available, a great deal of ingenuity is displayed to overcome difficulties and to bring Scout training to boys no matter where they are. Rover Crews are often run in Teachers' Training Colleges, thereby ensuring a steady flow of Teacher-Scouters. Where facilities exist, Air Scout Troops are formed, and many Sea Scout Troops flourish.

Opportunities for public service to the community and self-help are different in many countries from those in the United Kingdom. In some countries, the Scouts have undertaken projects to help villagers build improved sanitary arrangements, others have used their knowledge to build permanent bridges. Cases are known of Scout Troops building houses for old people and growing vegetables for them. In many places there are great religious festivals where hundreds of thousands of pilgrims gather together, and where the Scouts equip themselves to do special duties in first aid, care of children, feeding, and in other ways give help to those who attend.

In some parts of the Commonwealth there are natural hazards such as great floods, hurricanes, typhoons and cyclones, and the Scouts in those countries have on many occasions been able to render practical public service in times of devastation. In addition to helping others in such catastrophes, they have been able to assist in government schemes such as tree planting. Hundreds of thousands of trees have been planted by the Scouts of Kenya and Lesotho. Many Scout Troops have undertaken to keep the roads in repair around their schools, and on some islands in the Ellice Group, where all work is shared and it is hard to find anything of public service to do, the Scouts dig the graves and bury the dead—an unusual but practical good turn.

Every country has its own problems. They may be more or less than those in the United Kingdom, but in many parts they are very different. A number of Scouts have encountered lions while on their First Class hike. Cobras and rhinos have been unwelcome visitors at Scoutmasters training courses. Hyenas and leopards have wandered through Scout camps at night. One Scout said "It is difficult for me to be a friend to animals because a lion killed and ate my grandmother". Swimming is difficult in some countries where rivers are full of bilharzia and crocodiles, and man eating sharks infest the coasts. The Bob-a-Job system of fund-raising is not possible in all countries. Scouts have earned money to buy their equipment by making handicrafts, by vegetable market gardening, making copra, raising poultry and animals, and collecting empty bottles. At least one Troop in the Commonwealth collects subscriptions from its members in the form of coconuts. In many places boys suffer from malnutrition, or malaria may be endemic.

The provision of uniforms is often a problem, particularly in places where there is a subsistence economy. Uniforms vary to suit the climate, religious requirements, traditional dress and the economic standards of different countries. Official headgear includes the turban, beret, Scout hat, woven conical hat, and songkok, while in some places the Scouts wear no hat at all. In the same way that Scottish Scouts wear the traditional kilt instead of shorts, the Fijians wear the sulu, and the Gilbertese and Ellice Islander Scouts wear the lavalava. Alternative uniforms are permitted in some places, and in one country a Scout can be properly dressed wearing nothing but a scarf and a waistcloth. Some of the skills of Scout training are part of the life of the local people, and some boys are able, almost instinctively, to follow tracks made by men or animals, while others can trap and cook their own food before they join the Movement. For these, the tests in first aid or signalling are much more attractive. A boy's love of exploration and adventure is catered for in many ways. The Scouts of New Zealand and Australia regularly have expeditions into adventurous country, and the Scouts of Zambia have made journeys into Bechuanaland and found the "lost city of the Kalahari". Many isolated Groups carry out imaginative and worthwhile activities in the best traditions of the Scout Movement, under appalling difficulties. The leper Scouts of Makogai in Fiji, have built two boats with their own hands in order to camp on a nearby uninhabited island. The Scouts of New Zealand raised funds to buy engines for the two boats when they heard of the achievement, and as a result, the leper Scouts were able to add the care and maintenance of engines to their activities.

Communications and transport present difficulties and challenges. Camping, as popular in other parts of the Commonwealth as in the United Kingdom, often requires a great deal of organisation as well as walking. In the tropics it is usual to make shelters from natural materials instead of using tents.

In some countries firewood and water may be scarce. Food

supplies present problems, especially where fresh meat can very quickly go bad, and where the local diet consists of bulk food, difficult to buy locally or heavy to carry. However, if the boys are trained to accept difficulties as challenges and problems as opportunities, ways are always found to use to the full, the natural amenities available.

Because of government policy, many of the promising young men of the Commonwealth receive bursaries for further study in the United Kingdom, and a surprisingly large number of these are Scouters. While in the U.K. they are able to attend Scouter training courses and help in the running of Groups, and so further their own knowledge of Scouting and also contribute to the training of British boys.

We in the United Kingdom are proud of the fact that our Chief Scout is also the Chief Scout of the Commonwealth. As such, he has travelled extensively from the north of Scotland to the South of New Zealand, and from the Pacific Islands to the Caribbean islands, to meet the two million brother Scouts as their leader and friend.

There are many memorials to the Founder of Scouting. Many Baden-Powell Houses exist in the Commonwealth, and he is buried in a simple grave in Kenya. But he also has millions of living memorials, and the smiling bright eyes of youngsters throughout the Commonwealth are not the least of these.

6   DJBS

REMEMBER THE JAMBOREES?

"What else could you call them?" replied B.-P. when asked why. So far there have been eleven and, like saints, they've all been different. The twelfth is due to astonish the Scouting world in 1967, coinciding in dates with Brownsea Island.

They are not (contrary to the belief of some) organised exclusively by Great Britain, although the first, fourth and ninth were. It happens on this wise: that the World Conference mentions that in two years or so the time is coming round for another World Jamboree (supposed to happen every fourth year when the lunacy of mankind allows, although postponed from 1928 to 1929 because, of all reasons, 1928 was an Olympic Games year) and invites countries to offer as hosts. Considering what it costs to run (recent Jamborees apart from our own which cost a packet have all been sponsored or vastly aided visibly or invisibly by their governments) there isn't a rush to accept this honour, splendid though it is for prestige. Perhaps one day no country will offer and there'll be no more World Jamborees ...

The first in 1920 wasn't a Jamboree as we now think of it at all, but half Scout arena displays and half Scout handcrafts in practice, and wholly good public relations: added to which it proved once and for all B.-P.'s contention that when it came to Scouts they could work, play and live together whatever their colour, creed or anything else. It also acclaimed B.-P. Chief Scout of the World.

Copenhagen, Denmark 1924 set the pattern which by and large the rest were to follow: Scouts camping naturally together and learning the toleration and understanding that leads to friendship. Arrowe Park (England, 1929) celebrated the Scouts' coming of age (a year late as we see it nowadays), in the mud but with high spirits and a sense of achievement and a peerage for B.-P. which put Gilwell for ever on the map of the Scouting world. Gödöllö (Hungary, 1933) displayed its first Air Scouts and lavish hospitality; at Vögelensang (Holland, 1937) B.-P. prophetically said farewell to his Scouts.

Some were more elaborate than others: the French Jamboree at Moisson in 1947 is remembered, not only for the great heat of that summer or the forest setting, or the joy of seeing again Scouts from those countries whose Scouting had for years been practised underground, but for the elaborate opening by torchlight, the vast arena shows, the intricate closing hours. The Golden Jubilee affair in 1957 at Sutton Coldfield was even vaster, but it was a tripartite camp—Jamboree for Scouts, Moot for Rovers, Indaba for adults—the first and undoubtedly the last of its kind.

Before this, Bad Ischl (Austria 1951) had shown the joys of simplicity: "here", they implied "are lovely mountains and lakes, come and camp and be happy" and there never was a happier or less organised Jamboree: one evening an orchestra from Salzburg played Mozart by candlelight to entranced and wildly-encoring Scouts of many nations. There were storms too and some flooding, following the tradition of Copenhagen (where many Scouts had to emigrate from the camp to hospitable homes) and Arrowe Park and Sutton Coldfield (which one must expect in an English summer). On the other hand at Niagara (Canada 1955) one remembers the intense heat above all: it was to this Jamboree came the first great air lift of a thousand British Scouts. Fewer of them were to fly farther to Makeling Park (Philippines 1961) to an exotic camp at the jungle's edge; even more —1500—were to fly to Marathon (Greece 1964) to revel in the sea and the sunshine, and be educated without tears.

Perhaps Jamborees don't mean much except to those who attend them but those fortunate ones must surely have memories that will accompany them always.

SCOUTING THE WORLD OVER

I

In the beginning there were just Scout Troops. In the beginning too there were Scouts in the United Kingdom and nowhere else.

How then did it spread into other countries? There was no deliberate promotion, no public relations campaign, no emissaries going out to try and sell it and indeed so far as the United Kingdom was concerned no particular intention or desire that it should spread.

All the earlier growth was spontaneous, some through the grapevine of the boyhood of the world and some through foreign travellers who found in this island this new, unexpected and attractive thing and took it home to their own lands and talked about it and established it. Pioneers in very truth!

As it spread so the demands for B.-P., its originator and founder, to show himself in other lands grew with it and from a very early stage it became obvious that B.-P. accepted as one of the major tasks of his life this "showing himself" to the Scouting countries.

We need to look at two avenues of

growth; the first inside the British Empire, as it was, where the control of Scouting in such countries as Australia and Canada remained for many years very much the responsibility of Headquarters in London; and the growth into non-British territory where Scouting was never the responsibility of Britain except when requested in the capacity of adviser.

In the early years there was no international organisation of any kind. Organised world Scouting originated at the first Jamboree at Olympia in 1920.

At that Jamboree two very significant things happened. The leaders of the visiting contingents met together and felt the need for co-ordination and at the end of the Jamboree (what a moving and unforgettable sight it must have been) B.-P. was acclaimed as Chief Scout of the World—not elected, not appointed but acclaimed! There can have been few comparable occasions in the history of the human race. The magnificent account in *Two lives of a Hero** vividly presents the picture.

The next ten years saw much development throughout the world, not all of it successful, but in the majority of countries sound and enthusiastic beginnings were achieved and the Jamborees as they came around acted as springboards for further development and indeed for the spread of understanding. B.-P. continued to travel and he was inevitably and rightly the "hub of the wheel". In general terms it is fair comment that where growth was natural and spontaneous, success was achieved but where through Government or misguided enthusiasm Scouting was forced artificially, then the results were rarely so good and on occasion disastrous.

As Scouting spread, inevitably changes were found to be necessary in matters of programme and organisation and Scouting proved that it was capable of infinite flexibility. Indeed looking back I am one who believes that its expansion in many countries was hampered by an excess of loyalty in matters of detail to what was being done in the founder country. How inappropriate was a United Kingdom fire-lighting test to Australian boys and by what possible reasoning did some Southern Hemisphere countries adopt an Astronomer's Badge which included pointing out the North Star! How fatuous to have signalling tests for illiterate boys and swimming tests in near-

* Heinemann 63s.

Eskimo regions! However, there was much sense as well as nonsense in the spread and development to many countries. Europe took to Scouting from the very earliest stage and by 1939 it was well established in every country of any significance, apart from Russia (where the Scouting started in 1913 was a casualty of the revolution), and many of us can recollect with enormous pleasure the excellence of the Hungarian Jamboree.

The ability of the Scouts in the Baltic countries, sad to record, was lost with the other post-war Eastern European countries as the Iron Curtain moved westward and they had to abandon their Scouting under duress or on occasion under force.

It is not by chance that the enemies of freedom have always seen in Scouting a tremendous danger to their aims. The loss of Eastern Europe and more recently of Cuba and Burma are a real testimony to the essential rightness of Scouting as a buttress to the freedom of mankind. How strange that the enemies of freedom pay more attention to Scouting than do freedom's other friends.

The post-war years have seen a tremendous development in what in truth is geographically a smaller world, and the progress in Latin America where in earlier years National Scouting seemed to operate on the basis of stop–go has been solid, successful and effective. In Asia too, where in some respects Scouting is more needed than anywhere else in the world, they have learned the value and the effectiveness of the Movement, and the growth in such countries as Malaysia and Thailand has been both encouraging to Scouting and of immense value to the National interest. Much of Africa has evolved from dependence to independence which inevitably produces problems, yet one thing has become abundantly clear. Where under dependence Scouting was strong and purposeful then under independence it has tended to grow even stronger, whereas when under dependence the local Scout Movement was weak, under independence it has had an even harder struggle for survival. However, despite the problems, suffice it to say without any trace of complacency that the world strength of three million plus in 1939 has grown more than three fold to just short of eleven million in 1965 in a far smaller world.

II

World Organisation

As I have already said, the growth of the world organisation stems directly from the Olympia Jamboree. Shortly after there was established in London, where it remained until 1958, the International (now World) Bureau. Its purpose was to act as a co-ordinating Agency between the Scouting countries of the world, to be the servant of the World Committee and with that Committee to have an overall reponsibility for World Scout events and for the admission or rejection of new Scout countries.

The World Conference and the World Committee are democratic almost to a fault. Every country in the world has a right to send six delegates to each Biennial World Conference and each country has six votes irrespective of size, so that the Boy Scouts of America with its membership more than half the world total has no more voting strength than little Lichtenstein with its three hundred plus!

The Committee consists of twelve elected members with a maximum tenure in office of six years, not more than one may come from any one country. Men who, it is expected on election, will not attempt to represent their own country but will try to guide World Scouting as a whole and will try with the World Bureau and, as appropriate, Gilwell, to make known the successes and the failures of experiment and development, suggesting not that one method is better than another but trying always to make available knowledge of what is being done and attempted.

At the start it was no doubt inevitable that whatever existed should be accepted. Looking back it might have been considerably better if a firmer line had been taken at the outset. It might even have been possible to avoid the multiplicity of Scout Associations that still persist in many of the European countries with their consequent wastefulness of man-power and finance.

On the other hand, for many European countries it was and perhaps still is essential to have separate organisations based on religious interest or on occasion upon other, and to me less understandable, differences. My own feeling for what it is worth is that much progress has been hampered in the European scene by multiple Associations and it could be because of this that there has been very little numerical growth in Europe for many years. Sweden with six Associations, France with four, Holland and Denmark with two, might have proved even more successful than they have had it been said from the start of World Scouting: "one country, one Movement."

I must add a word about the relationship of Scouting, both National and International, with the religions of the world.

Many of us are too apt in my view to think of Scouting in Christian terms whereas the truth is that Scouting has spread because it has been found to be helpful and acceptable to all established religions, Christian and non-Christian. Indeed I have been proud to have been able to help Scouting develop in the Buddhist and the Moslem countries and I hope that the Leadership of Scouting will always hold the liberal views that B.-P. instituted and which have proved so right and so effective.

In essence the policy is this: Scouting as such is not concerned with what religion you profess but asks that you should accept and practise what you do profess.

III

Administration and Organisation

Inevitably the pattern of organisation that serves one country well is inappropriate to others. Broadly, at the Group level, there are two main conceptions, the one which for convenience one might call the British system whereby Packs and Troops are held together in a family relationship and the other used primarily by the United States and the Philippines where Groups as such are unknown and each unit whether Pack or Troop is an entirely separate entity with its own supporting committees, finance, etc.

Canada has a compromise between the two in the sense that it has Groups as Great Britain has but has no position for the Group Scoutmaster, the duties being performed by the Chairman of the Group Committee who is elected and not appointed.

There are other interesting and significant differences. In Great Britain and Australia every encouragement is given to a Group to own and develop its own headquarters; in the countries of North America the same thing *is actively discouraged, indeed to the point of being forbidden.* This situation underlines a great difference in conception. The British talk of a "Scout Movement" whereas the Americans offer and support a "programme"—to sponsoring institutions, churches, schools, Rotary and the like. The open Group as we know it is quite unknown in American Scouting; on the other hand the provision for permanent Camp Sites made in America is many, many times greater than happens elsewhere.

Then there is the enormous difference between the amount of professional full time help made available in individual countries. The American aim has for many years been one full time executive to every thousand members and so far as one can make a comparison (and that is by no means easy) the British equivalent probably works out like one to 20,000. All that one can say is that most countries in the world, and not least our own, are gradually realising that more professional help is essential if there is to be expansion and that intelligently handled professional help increases the need for voluntary help and secures it. For those (and there are some) who tend to be critical of the amount of professional help used in America it is surely worth facing the simple fact that proportionate to population they are at least three times as successful as we are. Put quite simply: one person in 25 is associated in some way or another with the Boy Scouts of America whereas in Britain it is one person in 90 and I can assure you it is not because the Americans like Scouting better than the British! It is simply that their organisation is able to sell the idea of Scouting both to adults and boys much better than we have ever done.

Many countries still do not permit women either to serve on committees or to help in the running of Cub Packs. In some cases it is due to tradition or to religion or it may be, and no doubt on occasion is, sometimes due to a country feeling that a boys' Movement should remain in the hands of men.

IV

Where and Why It Doesn't Exist

Scouting doesn't exist in the Iron Curtain countries as already indicated; in China, in Spain (although a growing unofficial Scout

Movement is apparent and there is a steady trickle of Spanish Scouters passing through Gilwell); in Cuba where Scouting struggled on bravely after Castro took over but shut down of its own volition because it found it couldn't remain a free agency and it had the courage to admit an impossible situation; Indonesia, officially still registered but there isn't really anything remotely resembling Scouting going on there at the present time; Burma, a very recent casualty and a sad one: in the words of its Government "The Movement is not in tune with a modern revolutionary state". Just what that remarkable statement was supposed to mean I have yet to discover.

V

Scouting's Contribution to National Life

The aim of Scouting the world over is identical and in a sentence can be described as "Trying to develop the character of boys through the application of the Scout Promise and the process of a stimulating programme", but its effect is different in degree and of necessity this must be so. In the majority of countries of Asia and Africa for example Scouting is almost exclusively an extension of the Education Service and the vast majority of Scoutmasters are school teachers: one reason for this is that the idea of voluntary unpaid service has never been established in these continents. This is in no sense critical of them for undoubtedly voluntary service as we know it takes many generations to develop.

On the other hand the immediate noticeable effects of good Scouting particularly away from the towns are most apparent in Africa than anywhere else I know. Camp Craft can lead to an immediate improvement in the living conditions in the kraal. Physical fitness developed through Scout games can have an instant effect and be most noticeable in comparing Scouts with their contemporaries, but perhaps above all the sense of belonging to something bigger than the immediate neighbourhood unit is effective and a rather wonderful thing to witness. I have heard few more moving sentences than that of a desert based Scout who told me that "Scouting has made the desert a beautiful place to live in".

Then in such a material thing as hut building Scouting has often raised the standard and whole villages are better housed because the boys are Scouts. Cooking standards too have often improved on the traditional standards.

These kind of benefits are apparent to any visitor, but beyond this, national life has been enriched by the corporate service rendered by Scouting in many many countries. Dealing with emergencies of flood and tempest or famine or indeed of war, the contribution of our own Scouts in the London blitz, in the Canvy Island flood disaster, in the Harrow train wreck; abroad in the Greek earthquake, the Indian famine, the West Indian hurricane, —in time of need in war or peace Scout training has proved itself time after time. And little things do count: when I asked the man in charge of the Canvy Island rescue operation why he was paying such tribute to the help given by Scouts, for there were many others trying to help, made the memorable reply "They were the only people who remembered to bring their own lunch".

The contribution of Scouts the world over would fill volumes: perhaps it is a pity the volumes aren't written; perhaps more public support would be in evidence if we had learned the virtues of more fervent trumpet blowing.

VI

The Editor has suggested that I should give my personal views about how I think World Scouting is likely to develop in the next 10 or 15 years and I do want to make it clear that the opinions I shall express are entirely personal tho' they are after all based on well over a million miles of travel in more than 90 countries.

I think inevitably Scouting as between one country and another will become increasingly different in terms of programme and in terms of organisation. Indeed, as I have indicated earlier I believe much progress in the first 50 years was hampered by the effort to apply a method and a programme that was designed for this country to places where it was often impossible and on occasion quite pointless. I have never in all the years I have been at Gilwell proclaimed unity of programme and the more I have travelled the more it has been borne in on me that this is neither feasible nor desirable. It is not only a matter of climate and terrain, those are obvious things, but it is also a matter of local custom and culture, of general educational standards, indeed on the degree of development. It is a matter too of what I would call differences of sophistication. There are, for example, many countries in the world where, because Scouting is still comparatively novel the Scouting of the 1920/1930s is appropriate and where the kind of pattern in which European countries, including our own, are making progress would be bound to fail. Yet I do see virtue in the unity as expressed in the World Conference Resolution of 1957, and I quote it in full:

"The Conference, as the central body of the Boy Scouts World Brotherhood, on the occasion of its Founder's Centenary and the Fiftieth anniversary of the birth of Scouting in the world, reaffirms its faith in the fundamental principles of Scouting as founded by the former Chief Scout of the World, the late Lord Baden-Powell of Gilwell:

1. Duty to God.
2. Loyalty to one's own country.
3. Faith in world friendship and brotherhood.
4. Accepting, freely undertaking and practising the ideals set forth in the Scout Law and Promise.
5. Independence of political influence.
6. Voluntary membership.
7. The unique system of training, based on the Patrol System, activities in the open air and learning by doing.
8. Service to others.

The Conference firmly believes that these principles, which have proved so successful, strongly contribute towards the formation of character in the boy of today, the man of tomorrow, to the great benefit of every nation, and through the spread of understanding and unity of purpose, of the world as a whole. May this be our endeavour in the strengthening of freedom and peace."

Surely these are the things that matter, not that all boys do the same thing or get a particular badge, not that Cubs use the Jungle background or don't use it, not that the kind of service that is encouraged and indulged in is identical. One of the service projects of a Latin American country is currently to wage war with an attack on illiteracy and inadequate sanitation which would be a pretty fatuous programme for a country like Switzerland.

There must too be differences in organisation and differences, as I have tried to show, in the quantity of full time professional help that a country needs. Where then is the common ground? Basically I think it is in the 1957 Resolution but one has to look a little further than this to the attitudes of many people in Scouting. No country is the custodian of all the good ideas, a group of persons even less. I think we must learn what I regard as the true spirit of Scouting, the spread of understanding and mutual respect, the making available of help when it is asked for and in the process all of us must get rid of any arrogant idea that the Scouting we do is necessarily exportable into different surroundings for use with quite different people. One of the untrue cliches that is uttered at countless conferences is this:

"Boys are the same the world over".

This is utter nonsense. All human beings evolve out of the environment into which they are born and in which they grow up. The environment of a modern sophisticated rat-race infested city just isn't the same as the environment of a jungle village or a desert kraal or even of a village in a highly civilised country. Consequently the boys are different because their environment is different and their needs are different because *they* are different.

Looking back over the years I realise increasingly that the true strength of Scouting lies in its sound principles which are universally applicable and the infinite flexibility through which those principles can be established. I look then to see increased flexibility of programme and I see the function of those of us involved with Scouting at the world level primarily of having the maximum knowledge of what is going on and then making the appropriate parts of that knowledge available where and when it is needed.

The purpose of Scouting can, and in my estimation should, always be the same but the method by which we seek to achieve the aim must be different if there is to be any universal success. Unity by all means but unity through intelligent divergence.

On the purely physical side I am not at all convinced that World

Jamborees in their present form are really worth the time and the effort and the cost. After all their direct effect on individuals is inevitably limited to a very tiny proportion of each country's membership and perhaps there is more merit in smaller and more frequent and more accessible gatherings and I would hope less grandiose international events.

I would like to see less nationalism but perhaps most of all I would like to see the adults in Scouting genuinely remembering that Scouting is for the boy. In short I would like to see Scouting concerned only with what it has to offer the boy of today. There is always virtue in limiting your objective to what is reasonably attainable.

Then I would like to see Scouting really grow. We proclaim truthfully if glibly about our ten million membership but in doing so we often forget that considerably more than half are in the United States and that 85 per cent of the total is in only ten countries. Those who proclaim that quality is preferable to quantity are usually seeking an excuse for their own lack of progress. The two things are not antipathetic for in all human endeavours true quality usually attracts quantity; this is as true of a Nation as it is of a Group.

Finally, I think many adults in Scouting are taking themselves too seriously, something B.-P. was never guilty of. To be serious about the enterprise is right but not when it becomes personal.

Now to conclude, the Editor has asked me to bring out of my memory two or three "traveller's tales", and I willingly accede to his request.

In Australia, a country for which I have the greatest affection and regard, I visited a Deputy Camp Chief who presided over one of the loveliest camp sites in the world on the Magnetic Island, which is situated off the north-east corner of Queensland. The heat was tremendous, the sands burning hot and I gladly sought the shade of the wooden office building, and it was there that my good friend addressed me in these terms:"This is the moment I have looked forward to, the day when you, the Camp Chief of Gilwell, would sit in my chair and in front of my desk". My reply obviously shocked him considerably, for it was this:"I am sorry, but that is one thing I am not prepared to do". The old man, near to tears, pleaded with me but I remained adamant. Finally he said, "Well, at least will you tell me why you won't sit in my chair?".

My reply, which I think was merited, was "because I don't much like the look of the snake wrapped round the beam above it". Our united exodus from the hut was remarkably agile.

A delightful site on a lakeside in the United States provides the setting for my next story. We were having a late night coffee around the camp fire when one of my American colleagues said, "I can't understand how it is that the mosquitoes don't seem to bother you, because they are driving me nearly mad". Now it is true that in recent years I have had very little trouble with insect bites. Maybe I was bitten so often earlier on that I am now inoculated, or perhaps I have now sufficient alchohol in my blood stream to keep them at bay. But that night, pulling his leg as I thought, I said, "Well, I have a system. Half an hour before I go to my tent I put a lighted torch inside it. The mosquitoes and other insects from a great distance around are attracted to it and I pull up the zip and let them fight it out for themselves, and I sleep under a bush". It didn't dawn on me that anyone would take such a statement seriously, and still less literally, but bless his heart he did, with a most surprising result. He followed my advice to the letter, and in the early hours of the morning we had the mother and father of a thunderstorm. His tent, in which he was not sleeping, was struck by lightning, and I suppose in a way my joke may possibly have saved his life, and certainly saved him from serious injury. But my word, he was wet and he was bitten!

At King's House, Jamaica—I enjoyed for a couple of days the splendid hospitality of the then Governor. A magnificent breakfast was brought to my room, curtains were thrown back and the glorious sunshine streamed in, and I think not unnaturally for an Englishman, I said to the servant, "Thank you—what a beautiful morning". His reply was memorable and courteously given: "And what Sir, did, you expect?"

And so to Surinam, and jungle country where on arrival in camp I was presented with a bucket and a long stick and was a little mystified until I went to the water hole and found that the stick was necessary to beat the water-snakes away, otherwise you would just get bucketfuls of snakes and very little liquid. From the same area, I remember the astonishing story of the Amerindian Scoutmaster who told me in all seriousness that his boys had to spend 48 hours unattended in the jungle before they were allowed to take the Tenderfoot test! I expressed my surprise and remember saying "But what happens if the boy gets lost or killed by a wild animal or snake?". The remarkable reply was "Well, that presents no problem, he would no longer be eligible for membership!" I became convinced that he meant every word of it!

Finally (for I could go on almost indefinitely) to Japan, and a lovely training ground, the central feature of which was the ancestral home of their late Chief Scout. I had been there three days before I realised that they were pulling my leg. It is a custom and a very good one, that when you enter a Japanese home you leave your shoes outside; but the difficulty that I had was finding my shoes when I went out to get them. The wretches were moving the doors, which is so easy in a Japanese house, and hiding round the corners and laughing at my problem. Indeed there was one occasion when a whole room vanished, a room in which I had put my jacket, which was solemnly handed to me later—but the room never reappeared.

There you are, a very small sample of thousands of memories and of a host of friends. The spirit of Scouting and the idea of brotherhood are real things and not just ideals. And it has really all happened because once, long years ago, a man wrote the simple phrase "A Scout is a brother to every other Scout, no matter to what country, class or creed the other may belong".

LAWS FOR ME WHEN I AM OLD.

I will have the poor people to be as rich as we are, and they ought so ought to be as happy as we are, and all who go across the crossings shall give the poor crossing sweeper's some money, and you ought to thank God for what He has given us and He has made the poor people to be poor and the rich people to be rich and I can tell you how to be good now I will tell it to you. You must pray to God when ever you can but you cannot be good with only praying but you must very hard to be good.

BY

R.S.S. Powell

Feb 26 1865

Robert Stephenson Smyth Powell

Written by Baden-Powell when he was aged eight

It was during the Siege of Mafeking that B.-P. first realised how well boys responded to responsibility being put on to them

On his return from South Africa, already the hero of many a boy, he was urged by Sir William Smith, Founder of the Boy's Brigade, to re-write his military handbook *Aids to Scouting* as a handbook for the training of boys. B.-P. felt that his theories first needed trying out in practice and at the beginning of August 1907 he held an experimental camp on Brownsea Island

In January 1908 *Scouting for Boys* was first published in a series of six fortnightly parts. Within weeks, Scouting had spread throughout Britain. In the same year the Scout Movement had spread to other lands . . . today there are nearly 8 million Scouts in almost 100 countries

The Acorn has indeed grown into a mighty Oak

H.M. George V arrives at the Windsor Rally

The Good Turn, "one every day", was taken seriously by the Scouts

Where 26,000 Scouts were reviewed by His Majesty

All good turns were
an adventure in 1910!

THE CAPTURE OF WINDSOR CASTLE
by the Boy Scouts, July 4th, 1911.

A famous cartoon by Bernard Partridge

THE KING'S RALLY IN PICTURES

On the 7th August 1920, as B.-P. mounted the dais to close the First World Jamboree at Olympia, a young voice proclaimed, "We, the Scouts of the World, Salute You, Sir Robert Baden-Powell, Chief Scout of the World!"

B.P. with Lord Somers, his successor as Chief Scout

Dear Scouts,

If you have ever seen the play *Peter Pan* you will remember how the pirate chief was always making his dying speech because he was afraid that possibly when the time came for him to die he might not have time to get it off his chest. It is much the same with me, and so, although I am not at this moment dying, I shall be doing so one of these days and I want to send you a parting word of good-bye.

Remember, it is the last you will ever hear from me, so think it over.

I have had a most happy life and I want each one of you to have as happy a life too.

I believe that God put us in this jolly world to be happy and enjoy life. Happiness doesn't come from being rich, nor merely from being successful in your career, nor by self-indulgence. One step towards happiness is to make yourself healthy and strong while you are a boy, so that you can be useful and so can enjoy life when you are a man.

Nature study will show you how full of beautiful and wonderful things God has made the world for you to enjoy. Be contented with what you have got and make the best of it. Look on the bright side of things instead of the gloomy one.

But the real way to get happiness is by giving out happiness to other people. Try and leave this world a little better than you found it and when your turn comes to die, you can die happy in feeling that at any rate you have not wasted your time but have done your best. "Be Prepared" in this way, to live happy and to die happy—stick to your Scout promise always—even after you have ceased to be a boy—and God help you to do it.

Your Friend.

The Lord Rowallan,
third Chief Scout
in 1959, made way
for Sir Charles
Maclean of Duart
fourth Chief Scout

Caring for all of God's creation is part of the Scout's way of life: here
Senior Scouts on an expedition rescue a lost lamb

"Little Lamb, who made thee?
Dost thou know who made thee?"

Tape recording bird song: you can't
be too young to begin, can you?

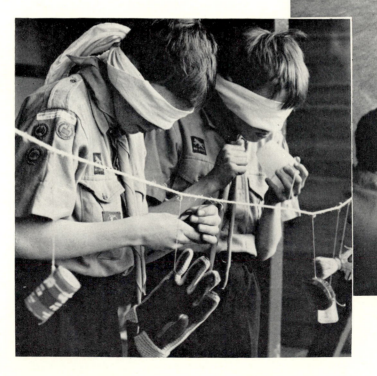

Although Scouting has a serious motive behind it much of the training is by means of games: training in observation (by touch and hearing as well as sight) develops from the famous Kim's game in Kipling's Book *Kim*

"Troop Night" is the weekly gathering for progressive training

Boys need activity and adventure; they need opportunities that help them to widen their horizons and to grow in courage; what is delinquency but achievement that has taken the wrong turning?

"Then it's Heigh for the nights that are spent in camp," the Scouts used to sing: camp with its challenge (as here in the Dead Man's Crawl) and its surprises (as the Scout waits for his clothes to dry!)

Scouts are explorers in
miniature: so they must
all know their rope-work

A boy cannot learn to face difficulties and dangers by sitting comfortably at home: the world awaits him. So Scouts seek adventure: canoeing has always been a joy and excitement for many

During the last twenty years caving (or pot-holing) has had a strange fascination for hundreds of bold and venturesome Scouts

"The days that make us happy make us wise," wrote John Masefield. "These are the days we shall dream about and we'll call them the good old days," wrote Ralph Reader. Many Scouts enjoy ambitious cooking in camp and are brilliant chefs in the making

Scouting is not an end in itself—or shouldn't be. A Scout trains himself
to be ready to act—with knowledge and skill—in an emergency. Since
Scouting began, in our country alone a Scout has saved someone's life
on an average every fifth day. These pictures are of an actual rescue
from Ben Lawers, Hertfordshire's Lochearnhead Scout Station

Any boy who wishes to—he may be blind or deaf or physically disabled—can become a Scout: "Scouts in spite of everything," the French call them. Some each year attend the Windsor Parade and here Queen Elizabeth talks to them

The Chief Scout,
Sir Charles Maclean,
at a reception (this
time at the Guild Hall
in 1966) where he
presents certificates
to Queen's Scouts

Her Majesty at Windsor, April, 1966

The Certificate reads:
"As a Queen's Scout you have
prepared yourself for
service to God and your fellow
men, and have shown yourself
a worthy member of the great
Scout Brotherhood, I wish you
God-speed on your journey
through life; may it prove for
you a joyous adventure"

"Now thank we all our God
   With hearts and hands and voices,
   Who wondrous things hath done . . ."

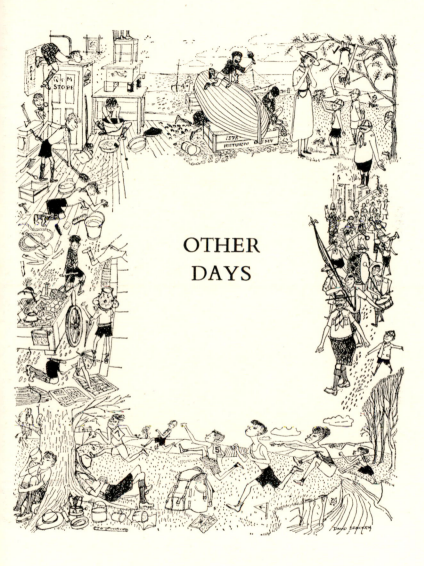

OTHER
DAYS

DJBS

OUR YOUNGEST LINE OF DEFENCE.

Boy Scout (to Mrs. Britannia): *"Fear not, Gran'ma; no danger can befall you now. Remember, I am with you!"*

["PUNCH": SEP. 1. 1909.]

From Richard Attenborough

I was a Wolf Cub thirty odd years ago, during the life-time, in fact, of our Founder, and on one never to be for-gotten occasion I had the thrill and honour of meeting the great man himself. I suppose of all the memories that one has of the eight or nine years in the Movement, that was probably the most poignant, but there are, of course, many others. My investiture when I took my Wolf Cub Promise, the tremendous excitement when I was appointed Senior Sixer, the first camp that I attended as a young Scout, my first solo hike and the day that I became a King's Scout (as it then was).

My debt to Scouting is immense, but it is no less to the two people who ran the 9th Leicester Group, May and Hubert Crofts. Mr. Crofts ran the Scouts and his wife the Cubs. Like so many Scouters and Lady Cub-masters throughout the world, they are the most dedicated and selfless people. Their whole lives, until their retirement, were bound up in the care and upbringing of young people and I am sure all of us who have had the benefit of people such as they can never ever repay the debt we owe them. For me it was they who suggested that I should take part in a Cub play—the first time I ever appeared in public. It was they who interpreted so lucidly and so fascinatingly the code by which members of the Movement are ex-pected to conduct their lives. A sense of service and a feeling of obligation towards others seems not to be of great importance these days. Indeed, such sentiments tend to be thought of in some quarters as somewhat "square". Well, if that be so, then I was a square thirty years ago and I am, I hope, still a square today.

I firmly believe that the Boy Scout Movement is the greatest Youth Movement ever devised, holding, as it does, the opportunities of every form of activity for which a boy could wish and, provided its ideas continue to expand and progress, while always holding on to it's precious traditions, I can see no reason why it should not continue to live up to the great ideals set by it's Founder.

Certainly, for me, the happiest and the most rewarding times of my youth, when not with my family, were spent with the 9th Leicester Group of which I had the great honour, ultimately, to be Troop Leader.

From Christopher Chataway

I was a Cub and then a Scout between the ages of eight and thirteen. It was a compulsory activity at the school I attended, and that is not I suppose looked upon as the ideal arrangement in these days. But my Scouting memories are wholly happy ones.

My imagination was certainly captured by what I may now deferentially describe as the mystique and the paraphernalia of the business. I enjoyed the challenge of passing tests; it was the same kind of individual challenge that led me later to athletics. And I was immensely excited both at the prospect and the reality of camping.

Perhaps the prospect was best of all. I can remember staring dreamily out of classroom windows on hot summer afternoons thinking of life in a tent. Happy hours were stolen from Latin, divinity, and French grammar, as I worked out menus and lists of equipment in sly corners of odd exercise books. As the end of term approached, and one awaited the day of departure on a camping expedition to the New Forest, one knew such an agonised expectancy as no event, whatever its personal importance, can possibly arouse in later life.

Although the camp itself could never of course quite live up to these expectations it was a wonderful experience all the same, and an experience from which I now recognise that I gained a great deal.

At my next school there was no Scouting. So I never became a First Class Scout, and perhaps missed what may be potentially the best years in the Movement. I am sure that many young people will continue to derive enormous benefit and pleasure from Scouting and I wish the Movement every success in its Diamond Jubilee Year.

From the Rt. Rev. the Bishop of Gibraltar

I am very glad to be able to write something for the Diamond Jubilee Book about my Scouting days which began just after the First World War began in 1914. I was rather old to begin (15 years of age) but I was at once fascinated by the Movement. My Patrol Leader was a year or so older than I and we began a deep friendship, ended by his death in France in 1918. My first camp was at Whitsuntide 1915. I had become an Instructor by that time. It began as most of my camps did with torrents of rain and soaking tents and kit! After the summer camp that year I spent the rest of my school holidays helping in Scout uniform in Canteens in munition works. From that time onwards I was in Scouting actively until 1931. I even managed to do some while serving in the army (1917–1918).

When I was ordained I had the joy of starting a Troop in my first parish in Croydon. One of the most thrilling experiences to me as a G.S.M. and a priest was my last summer camp with that Troop (of course it began with heavy rain). We were camping near Portsmouth and I was able to take the boys all over that great battleship, H.M.S. Hood, (so tragically sunk with all hands during the last war). But the great moment was our Holy Communion Service each Sunday and on the last day of camp. Forty one out of the forty two in camp received Holy Communion out in the open with an improvised altar. My last Camp was in 1929 when my wife and I took our respective Wolf

Cub Packs to Seaford. Oh yes! we were soaked as we pitched tents, had to sleep that night in a school and then had nine glorious days of sunshine.

I thought then, and still think, that Scouting holds the greatest potential for the development of the very best in boys and young men, provided that it has a definitely religious background. Baden-Powell was so absolutely right when he made the First Law—A Scout is loyal to *God* and the king. His aim was to make Scouts into "whole" people—Soul, mind, body.

May Scouting never lose its ideals and may it have a long and glorious future.

+ Stanley Gibraltar

From the Rt. Hon. Lord Hill of Luton

I joined the 51st South London Troop in 1914 at the tender age of ten. Mercifully there were no Wolf Cubs in those days so, by popping a year on my age, I was accepted.

Then, after an uneasy start, I climbed the usual ladder of Second, Patrol Leader, Second Class Badge, First Class Badge and King's Scout.

How I loved those beautiful badges and that golden cord! And I played the bugle or, to be more accurate, I blew into it and some terrible noises came out.

But this bare recital of those Scouting years means little in itself. For at least five years Scouting came first in my life. Tuesday, Thursday, Friday, Saturday and Sunday were Scouting fixtures every week, with Easter, Whitsun and Summer camps in Epping Forest as extras. As soon as one was over, I looked forward to the next.

What Scouting did for me is difficult to express. That it was the most exciting and absorbing feature of those youthful years I have no doubt. Scouting meant work, play, fun, fellowship—all the things that a lad needs. It gave one an enthusiasm and I suspect Scouting provides just those things which, whether they know it or not, so many lads need today. There may be less opportunity for wood-craft and for those rustic skills at which Baden-Powell so excelled. But that there is no less a need for the idealism, the inspiration, the fellowship and the fun of Scouting today than there ever was I cannot and do not doubt.

From Jimmy Logan

I am one of a Show Business family. Before the war my mother and father used to take the family to Bangor in Northern Ireland. They would take over one of the local halls, build a stage, add in lights and seats, and present their own show. At 8 years of age I was selling the programmes, chocolates and cigarettes, and all my summer holidays were concerned with the Theatre. But, there came a time when mum and dad had to tour the country, and so one of my brothers, my younger sister and myself went to live in Gourock on the River Clyde, with an aunt and uncle, who lavished on us the love they would have given their own children.

It was there, in 1941, I first took an interest in Scouting, and became a member of the 1st Gourock 6th Renfrewshire Boys' Scouts. I remember the excitement when my uniform arrived: the shirt seemed to be stiff enough to stand upright of its own accord, and the belt shining and smelling of new leather. We used to camp at the weekends at Inverkip, and I would cycle from Gourock to spend a week-end at camp. You can always tell a young Scout who has never camped before: his kit bag is usually twice as big as he is, loaded with frying pan, pots and that great instrument, the knife fork and spoon all clipped together. I certainly remember leaving behind the impression that I would be gone for at least a month instead of two nights. I remember vividly my first experience of a Pup tent, in the rain, lying on my stomach, frying sausages at the tent door, only to discover the flame from the Primus Stove had burnt a large hole in the flap of the tent, and somehow or other there seemed to be a large pool of water under the ground sheet. We were a small Troop, and suffered severely from the fact that the local Boys' Brigade had their own Pipe Band; we had nothing as glamorous, just a love of Scouting.

I became a member of the E.R.O. (Emergency Relief Organisation): they were responsible for stocking the local schools and halls with blankets and paraffin lamps and heaters for emergency use in case the local population were bombed out of their homes. I was their one, and if I remember correctly, their only messenger. We operated from the office of the Registrar of Births, Marriages and Deaths, and I was issued with what was then recorded as a sign of authority and position, a steel helmet. Proudly I carried this strapped on to my shoulder, in case I should be at a Scout Meeting, and we should be caught in the middle of a German raid. I'm afraid this practice ceased, when in a moment of frivolity one of the Scouting brothers pushed me. I stumbled back and the steel helmet went right through a chip-shop window. Shaking like a leaf I confronted the owner of the shop, so perhaps that early incident helped me to face up to my responsibilities.

Eventually the day came when I reached the dizzy heights of Patrol Leader. When I left the Scouts, I went into show business full time, and after various experiences, began to gain some success as a Comedian. One night in the Paisley Theatre, they told me that Ralph Reader was in front; he never came back-stage, but every year when he came North to Scotland, Ralph asked where I was playing and came to see the Show. Years later when we met I discovered that he had followed my career and taken an interest in my success, then we became firm friends. He was at that time to me a great star, and it was a thrill to know he was in the audience. It was even a greater pleasure to meet him years later and confirm my original opinion of him.

The world needs Scouting. A little of the lessons of Scouting rubs off on every boy, the pride, the comradeship, the use of initiative, particularly the opportunity for the town boy to see the country, all this is part of growing up, it gives a boy a standard to live up to.

It is a memory of the past that becomes a background for the future.

From Brian Rix

I was both honoured and somewhat amazed to receive an invitation to contribute an article for inclusion in the Diamond Jubilee Book, for it is with much regret that I must tell of my youthful shortcomings and admit I was not a *very* good Scout. The Scout motto is "Be Prepared", and I was ever far from prepared! In mid-1965, when Sir Charles MacLean first approached me on the subject of this article, so unprepared was I that in fact it has taken me until 1966 to put pen to paper. This display of disobedience towards one's superiors in Scouting is perhaps the best illustration of why I should not really be included in this book at all!

The Scout Movement, by way of its method of character building and development of initiative, has helped in no mean way to produce many fine personalities, but the following paragraph will show that my initiative, already highly developed, was directed almost exclusively to finding the loopholes in knots, rather than tying the knots themselves!

Perhaps it was my sense of theatre and the basic idea of dressing-up which first sparked-off my desire to join a Troop. It was with great excitement that I snipped with scissors (I had neither knife nor knowledge of tying or untying at this tender age) the string on the carton containing my uniform. In fact, in those early days, the uniform was everything, and worn with considerable pride. This did not last very long as, at that time, the rough grey shirts worn caused endless itching, and my three-finger salute was more often directed, not at the temple, but at some point of irritation! In spite of this, I became so much "up to scratch" (bad joke!) that I was eventually promoted to Troop Leader! (On reflection I am certain there was an element of "fiddle" here: by coincidence I was Head Boy at the Preparatory School to which the Scout Troop was attached, and I'm sure it was a matter of internal politics that whoever was Head Boy automatically became Troop Leader.)

The outdoor life has never attracted me, with the exception of continually attempting to barbecue my body in the hot Mediterranean sun, although as a Scout I did attend Camp; in fact I am probably one of the few Troop Leaders to have slept in a warm, comfortable feather bed, while all other ranks were ear-deep in mud! As a child I had continual ear trouble, and it was part of the arrangement that when at Camp I should bunk-down at a farmhouse adjacent to the neat rows of bell tents.

On two occasions I remember well I managed to win the prize for fishing trout. This I carried off by the dubious means of setting night-lines, and dispensed with the boredom of watching a float! However, they were happy days and remembered with affection. Perhaps I am painting far too gloomy a picture of my boyhood, for out of the Movement I have gained a number of assets which have proved useful over the years. At least my Brownie daughter, Louisa, can boast that her father was a Troop Leader—I sincerely hope she will not read of my exploits!

Good luck and greetings to Scouts everywhere.

From Field-Marshal Sir Gerald Templer, K.G., G.C.B., G.C.M.G. & C.

I am very proud of my enrolment card into the Dog Patrol of the 1st Shrewsbury Troop of Boy Scouts. I have it still and it is dated September 1908, which is quite a long time ago and only a few months after this great Movement first started. I'm afraid I wasn't a very distinguished or efficient Scout. I have only two clear recollections of that time. The first was taking my cooking test. I made an Irish stew which was apparently considered good enough for the award of my badge. I had certain doubts about it myself and gave it to our dog—an Irish terrier. Knowing what was what, he was promptly sick. The second recollection is a good deal more important. Scouting as a small boy of ten gave me lots of interest, plenty of fun and excitement and I think a sense of romance engendered I am quite sure by B.-P.'s book "Scouting for Boys" and its delightful illustrations.

Off and on throughout my subsequent life I have actively interested myself in Scouting—in the slums of York and later in the lovely Wiltshire countryside. And during my time as High Commissioner of Malaya, in the bad days of the Emergency, I tried to take my duties as Chief Commissioner of Malaya as seriously as the time available to me allowed. I learnt at first hand in that country what so many other Scouts have learnt before and after— that Scouting can indeed be a great catalyst between boys of different races and backgrounds, of different religions and of different colours. To attend some Scout affair in that lovely country at that difficult time indeed did one's heart good, and gave one courage to pursue the illusive objective of trying to produce a truly multi-racial society, —an objective which B.-P. himself would so strongly have approved.

We live in times of tremendous change, and certainly Scouting has to adjust itself to modern requirements. That is as it should be—provided always that happiness, excitement, romance, together with the teaching of duty and service remain as its primary objectives. I am sure they will.

I owe a great deal to Scouting. I have given it so little in return.

From the Rt. Rev. the Bishop of Warrington

My earliest memory of Scouting goes back to the First World War. One of my uncles was a District Commissioner, and his son a young Scouter (I think one of his daughters was too—what days they were!). I joined a Cub Pack in 1916 or 1917, and achieved the dizzy rank of Senior Sixer, with three gold rings on my arm. This was in Bedfordshire, and I have a clear recollection of what seemed like a great rally to meet the Chief (B.-P. of course) at Luton Hoo. The Chiltern Hills between Luton and Dunstable were our local jungle, and the thrill of my first Scout camp in 1920 by the muddy banks of the Ouzel is still with me. Then there was the golden summer of 1921, when I slept at the District standing camp for the best part of three months, and learned to swim in a muddy pond we used for bridge-building. Our headquarters was in what had been a hen-run, at the top of our Scouter's garden. He was Stanley Bennett, immortalised to thousands of Bedfordshire Scouts as Beano, and marvellously active until he reached his eighties. Another great local figure was Ernest Scott, the outstanding parson-Scouter of my boyhood. The rally at Alexandra Palace to welcome home the Prince of Wales from abroad is another highlight, coloured by the memory of being put under the railway-carriage seat by my travelling companions when they had enough of my chatter. But the most glorious experience was the Copenhagen Jamboree in 1924, which I attended as a member of the Bedfordshire composite Troop. Now

I began to understand what a big and splendid thing Scouting really was.

It was when I was near to gaining my First-class badge that the Troop was bereft of Scouters, and for a time, as Troop Leader, it fell to me to hold the Troop together. Thank goodness it wasn't for long, but at seventeen I was acting-A.S.M., and had completed most of my Wood Badge at nineteen. Some of the mud of Arrowe Park will probably cling to me until my dying day, but it was fun, as a Cambridge University Rover, to be one of the camp police, even though water bailiff would have been a better description. Soon I was to become a parson-Scouter, first in South London, then back to Bedfordshire, and Hertfordshire. As another war took all my Scouters away, I found myself running an inflated Troop and two Cub-Packs. I doubt if I shall ever again have such a feeling of relief as on those evenings when Cub duties were done, and seven days intervened before the next agony had to be endured! Somehow we managed to keep camping alive, at Knebworth, Tewin Water, and once beside an R.A.F. station to which I ministered. And when the war was over there was that memorable Jamboree at Moisson, in war-shattered France, surely the greatest triumph of improvisation some of us will ever see.

What do these memories of fifty years add up to? Out-of-doors delight in simple things. An incomparable if sometimes amateur training in "Do-it-yourself" at all sorts of curious levels. A vast amount of fun, and plenty of physical exertion—toiling up to Boar's Hill, above the dreaming spires of Oxford, towing a grossly overladen trek-cart, clambering up the rocks and sliding down the screes of Lakeland, cycling round my beat as District Commissioner visiting troops and packs in war-scarred South London. And knowing myself to be part of a comradeship infinitely varied, embracing boys and men of all sorts and sizes, all races and religions, held together by a common code which all could understand. Getting to know a succession of men who had learned much, and so had much to give.

And what of the future? If only Scouting can capture the loyalty of men of this and future generations who are of the same stamp as those who moulded Scouting into what it has become, I have no doubt that it will live on, and be re-shaped to serve many new generations of boys the world over. Its code of life, and its urge to adventure, will counter-balance the sterile influences of our increasingly urbanised, mechanised and de-personalised society. And its spirit of brotherhood may yet prove to be a large part of the answer to the problems of a world of reluctant neighbours.

+ Laurence Warrington

From the Prime Minister,
the Rt. Hon. Harold Wilson

To look back on my own connection with the Scout Movement is to look back on a medley of nostalgic and often humorous memories.

There was the time I was gloriously sea-sick on a cut-price trip to Holland. There was the time I nearly poisoned some of my fellow Scouts by serving them cabbage cooked with washing soda instead of cooking soda; that, of course, was really the fault of one of the junior Scouts! And there was the ingenious electric camp fire—rigged up with red paper and light bulb by the group's shadow Minister of Technology—around which we squatted hopefully chanting: "Burn, fire, burn."

My memories of Scouting are many because I came to Scouting so early. I joined the Wolf Cubs the week before my eighth birthday; the regulations had to be bent a little for that, but I was determined to join too early rather than too late. My father rose as high as District Commissioner. I began as a Wolf Cub in the 3rd Colne Valley Group, and ended up a King's Scout in the 28th Birkenhead Group. But even after my active Scouting came to an end in 1934 I kept up the link, and when I entered the House of Commons I was proud to become a member of the Houses of Parliament branch of the Guild of Old Scouts.

For me, my Scouting days were a golden time of comradeship and challenging activity, and many of the friends

I made as a Scout are still friends today. But what remains with me is the simple but valid philosophy I learned in the Scout Movement. In particular I shall always remember the sermon a Rover once preached on the text: "He has made of one blood all nations that dwell upon the earth." It was that sermon which engendered the attitude towards the evils of racialism which I still hold today.

It is in establishing among the youth of the nation an ethos of service and constructive idealism that, in my opinion, the future of Scouting in this country lies. The Welfare State can and should deal with the material problems of poverty and hardship. But the human aspects—the abating of loneliness, the need for odd jobs to be done about the house—are often best left to voluntary organisations. And among those organisations the Boy Scout Movement, with its special, unique tradition of the Good Turn, has an indispensable part to play.

Harold Wilson

"The boss said don't hurry
back — a ten year old Boy
Scout is doing your job"

CAMP

I write of the sun falling across the field,
The boys in shining shirts, and barefooted,
Cross to the farm, through the yellow dust of the flowers,
To fetch white milk cool in the clanking cans.
In the high noon they rested; the hot smell of blankets,
The grains of grass tickle the soles, and senses.
At tea they roll down the slope, clasping their towels;
The scratches sting in the salt water of the pool;
The rock is hard, and cold, for the unsteady feet.
The brown faces, the fresh water-washed limbs;
The boys go softly back to their camp home.
Now cricket and climbing trees or cutting wood;
The shade spreads; the evening voices are sweet
On the distant air. The smoke of the fire rises.
Muffled in jumpers, they contend with the dew. Supper
Under the cherry tree, clamour, then bowed heads
For Grace. Darkness comes soon and silently to the field.
The fire flames red, they crouch round it.
Their voices fly up in songs both sad and glad.
The story falls on ears not far from dreams
And sleep. At last, God blessed, goodnight, goodnight.

G. Cunningham

"Now, it says 'wind neatly round a green, peeled stick.'"

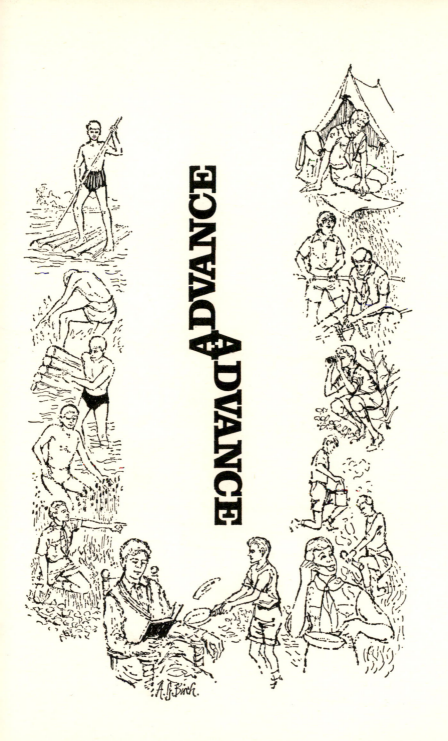

ADVANCE ADVANCE

A.J.Birch.

ALMOST all, if not all of our contemporary readers, but not necessarily all those future readers who may take down this book from the shelf and derive pleasure and information from it, will be aware that in January 1964, a body of 24 selected younger Scouters met for the first time at the request of their Chief Scout, Sir Charles Maclean, to study all aspects of Scouting's future. Two years later, to the month, they had ended their vast deliberations and were ready to present the results of their incredible industry (all, it must be remembered, in their leisure hours) in a report to the Chief Scout which they did on the 19th February, 1966.

They had considered thousands of letters from the Movement and from people of all walks of life; carried out experiments and research; interviewed people whose views, critical and otherwise, were important to their review; visited conferences and camp sites and taken every opportunity of finding out just how Scouting should, in their opinion, be shaped for the years ahead. The Chief Scout's Advance Party, as this body was called, met in full concert on seven weekends but the various committees into which for working purposes the members formed themselves met on 166 occasions. They studied methods used in other countries; one member travelled to Australia, New Zealand, Canada and the United States of America.

In June 1966 the Reports in a full size and a more concise popular form were published. The recommendations they made covered everything about our Movement—its Law and Promise, the age ranges and programmes of the Training Sections, the appointment and training of Scouters, organisation of Scouting at every level and so much more. At the same time the Committee of the Council, the governing body of the Scout Movement, published its decisions on the recommendations. The National Commissioners' Conference at Manchester University in the September had the report as its theme. It was a root and branch investigation.

Whatever has now been decided, the Report of the Advance Party marks the end of the era—as this Jubilee Book does. This book although not pretentious or too ambitious, or a complete history or final assessment is a small souvenir to mark an occasion —a birthday, recognition of sixty wonderful years.

If by their deliberations the Advance Party can bring as much happiness to so many boys, can help Scouting to achieve as much in the second sixty years as it has achieved in the first sixty years, it will indeed have deserved the greatest gratitude of all concerned—of boys and young men, their parents, their friends and their country.

So now: with high hearts and resolute hopes let us advance to the years ahead!

"And then I said to him 'Well, Chief, if you want my advice . . .'"

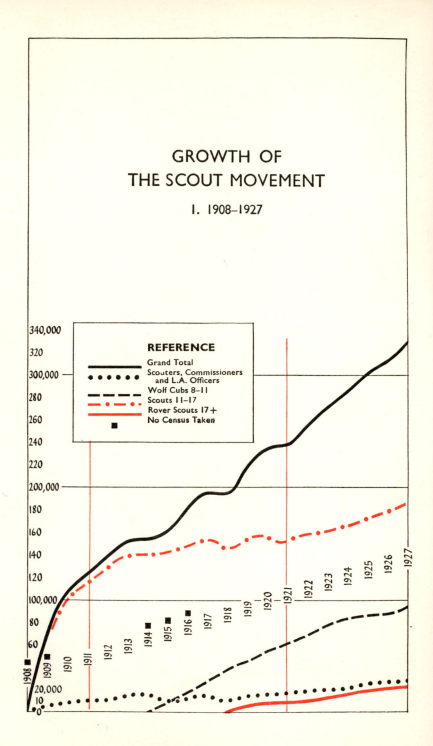

GROWTH OF
THE SCOUT MOVEMENT

I. 1908–1927

REFERENCE

Grand Total
Scouters, Commissioners
and L.A. Officers
Wolf Cubs 8–11
Scouts 11–17
Rover Scouts 17+
No Census Taken

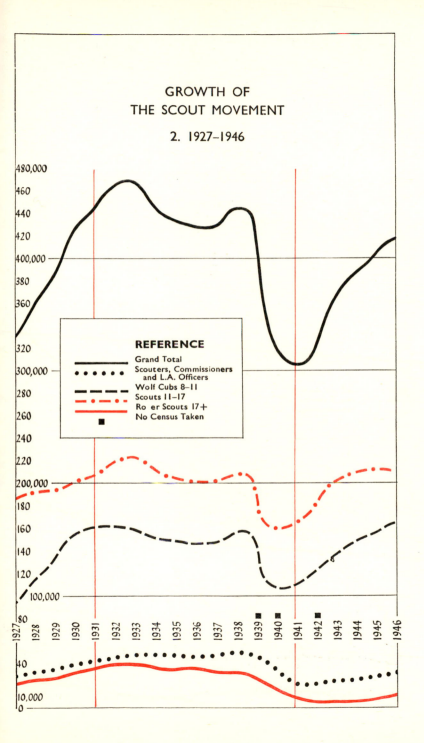

GROWTH OF
THE SCOUT MOVEMENT

2. 1927–1946

REFERENCE

Grand Total
Scouters, Commissioners and L.A. Officers
Wolf Cubs 8–11
Scouts 11–17
Ro er Scouts 17+
No Census Taken

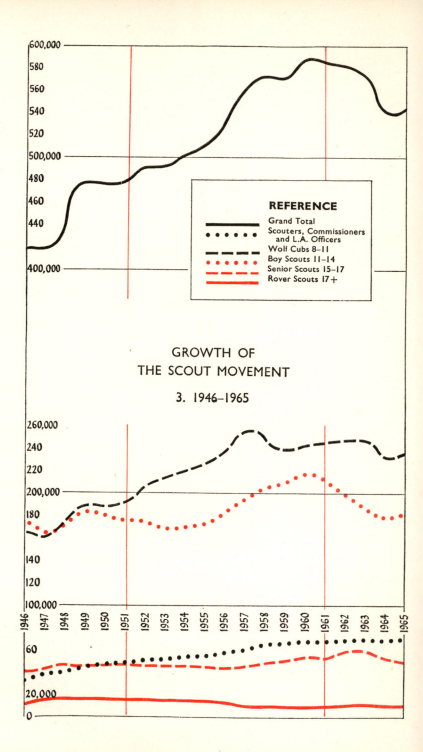

REFERENCE

Grand Total
Scouters, Commissioners and L.A. Officers
Wolf Cubs 8–11
Boy Scouts 11–14
Senior Scouts 15–17
Rover Scouts 17+

GROWTH OF
THE SCOUT MOVEMENT

3. 1946–1965

Time present and time past
Are both perhaps present in time future
And time future contained in time past.

(Four Quartets: "Burnt Norton")